# S.H.O.R.T.S.*

*Some Humorous Opinions Regarding Today's Society

1-800 465-1212

by Jack Lacy

Library of Congress Catalog Card Number: 95-90332


ISBN: 0-9643918-0-5


This book was published by Triple J Press. The book was prepared for publication and produced by Alpenrose Press. To order by mail, please contact the publisher.



Editor:              Mary Ellen Gilliland
                     Alpenrose Press
                     P.O. Box 499
                     Silverthorne, CO 80498
                     (970) 468-6273


Cover Design:        Hank Parker Illustration
                     P.O. Box 2811
                     Dillon, CO  80435
                     (970) 468-2632


Publisher:           Triple J Press
                     3154 E. Long Circle South
                     Littleton, CO  80122
                     (303) 779-0033

# CONTENTS

## *Air Travel*

Traveling by airliner is the only way to go--but first you must adjust your attitude toward taxi cabs. Have you noticed that every year it costs less to fly to Europe--and more to get to the airport?

When you get into a cab these days, the first thing you see is a half-dozen home-made signs, "Thank You For Not Smoking." "No Change Made For Bills Over $5.00." "Do Not Slam The Door." "Do Not Litter The Floor!" "Do Not Open Window While Air Conditioning is On." We used to have cab drivers. Now we have mothers-in-law with meters.

I'm having a special badge made just for riding in taxicabs. It says, "Thanks For Not Asking Me Not To Smoke." It bothers me when I'm sitting in a cab that's getting 22 miles to a quart of oil, and the driver's telling me not to smoke. You pay for his air pollution through the nose. Once you get to the airport you can relax. You have completed the most dangerous part of the trip.

Some people are afraid of flying, which is ridiculous. What you have to be afraid of is falling. I was in a helicopter once and the blade fell off. I asked the pilot, "Is it serious?" He said, "Not this time, because we're still on the ground. But if it happens again....!"

It's hard to believe these new planes will be able to stop on a dime--providing they're placed at the end of a 10-mile runway. One of them needs so much space to land, they've ruled out Rhode Island.

I could never understand why anyone flies first class. It costs you a fortune and all you get is a free drink, a wider seat, and the privilege of being first on the mountain when something goes wrong.

Air travel has become the greatest passenger service on earth. Everybody is airborne, and the airports are busy. The Chicago air traffic is severe. We were stacked over the city so long that the plane became obsolete.

Thanks to the airplane a typical vacation is a 14-day, five-country tour, followed by a 24-payment, two-year loan!

## Art

You can read anything you want to believe into a work of art. I like that picture of Whistler's mother 'cause it really tells a story. Here's this old lady--waiting for the TV set to come back from the repair shop. Or maybe she's just rockin' and waitin' for Whistler's father to come home from the bistro. If you think Whistler's father was forgotten, how about the chef for the "Last Supper?"

Then there's the Mona Lisa; she can tell you lots of things. She looks like your wife does when you say you had to work late at the office. A lot of people are fascinated by the sly, questioning smile. Not me. I see it every year on the face of my tax examiner. In a way, it's amazing the popularity Mona Lisa has. Through the years, tens of millions of people have gone out of their way to see this girl--who in real life couldn't make it in a singles bar. She has the expression of a reporter listening to a politician.

Artists have a tough time with critics. I was reading the story of Michelangelo, the Italian painter, who spent seven years painting the Sistine Chapel. Just think! Seven years to get a ceiling painted. They must have the same landlord I do. He didn't mind the seven years so much. What bugged him was when they asked for a second coat.

As luck would have it, Michelangelo finished his masterpiece, climbed down from the scaffolding, and the very first person he ran into was his mother-in-law. She looked up at the ceiling, looked at him, and said, "From this you make a living?"

## *Auto Mania*

I don't care what the chemistry books say, the principal by-product of petroleum is poverty. The biggest problem facing motorists today is whiplash. You get it from watching the price of gas go up. Our friendly neighborhood gas station is now known as the Bermuda Triangle. It's where $20 bills go and are never seen again.

I've always been confused by the term "crude oil". I don't know whether it refers to the grade of oil or the method of pricing.

Americans aren't about to quit driving their cars. An automobile is, of course, a marvelous fusion of metal, glass, wire, rubber and fabric. But it is much more than that.

It is the young man's wings, and the old man's limbs; it is the doctor's motor of mercy; a magic carpet for the

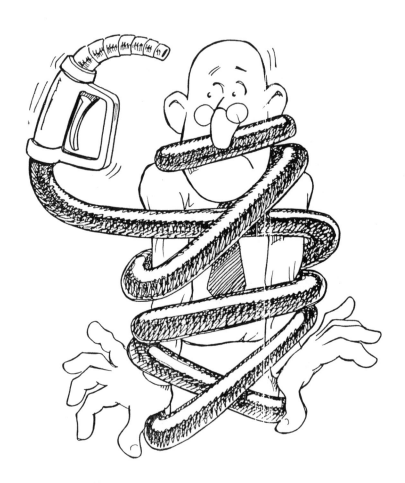

family with a vagabond heart; the sportsman's trail to fish and game; the merchant's messenger; a miracle on four wheels that binds the nation together; the maker of highways and the greatest pioneer since Dan'l Boone. It is, in the mind of its maker, the greatest achievement of utility and beauty in the history of mankind; it is, in the mind of its final owner, a lifeline of convenience, comfort, adventure, and happiness.

That's why we Americans will continue to patronize those one-arm bandits known as serve-yourself stations. Where else but in America can you see people making $25,000 a year pump their own gas, while a kid gets paid $4.50 an hour to sit on a stool and watch them?

One analyst said, "Price cuts earlier this year helped rekindle consumer demand and set the stage for price increases." Maybe when they jack up the prices, we should jack up our cars!

## *Babies*

The world registered its biggest 12-month population increase in recent history and reached 4,721,887,000 people by mid-June--a one-year increase of 82,077,000 people. That's a *lot* of babies!

Apparently people in China, India, the Soviet Union, and Indonesia aren't watching U.S. television or reading U.S. newspapers. They're not getting our daily message concerning abortion, birth control, and sex education.

Having babies seems to be an institution bigger than politics. All of the hand-wringing and lobbying hasn't been a very effective contraceptive.

Babies have been around for a long time and it appears they'll be around for some time to come. Raising kids is like eating grapefruit. No matter how you do it, the little squirts get to you.

They say there's something about having a baby that changes night into day--and that's true. It's called the Two O'Clock Feeding. Babies are nature's way of showing people what the world looks like at 2 a.m.

Feeding a baby is simple if you remember one thing: Everything that goes into a baby's mouth has to be boiled. Which is why bottle-feeding has become so popular. However, you can always tell the difference between a first baby and the ones that come after. For the first baby you buy a $65 sterilizer and a bottle is never put in his mouth until it's boiled for two hours. But by the time the fifth baby comes along, it's a little different with the bottle. He's sharing it with the dog.

Babies are very delicate. When you pick up a baby, everyone says, "Hold the head!" I know why--it's the safest part. If you pick one up, you have to hold the head to keep from breaking his neck. When they become teenagers you have to hold your temper to keep from doing likewise.

I love to go down to the maternity hospital and sit in

the waiting room. You hear fascinating conversations. One woman came out with her new baby and her husband was taking her home. She turned to her husband and said, "Now will you believe those pills were aspirin?"

Babies just seem to have a way of sneaking up on us. Is that really so bad?

## Back To School

One drug store really knows how to merchandise. They are running a "Back to School Sale" on notepaper for the kids, and a "Back to School Sale" on Valium for the teachers. It's the restraint teachers must exercise that drives them nuts.

When I was a boy we had a teacher who used to whack you on top of the head with a ruler. She phoned my father one day and said, "I'm sorry, but you know your son just isn't doing very well in class this year." My father said, "Gee, I know, I think he's got brain damage. Someone's been hitting him on the head with a ruler." One time I told the teacher, "I don't want to scare you, but my father said if I didn't get better grades someone is due for a licking!"

Between the discipline at home and the discipline at school we managed to get a healthy dose of the "Seven R's" Reading, 'Riting, 'Rithmetic, Reasoning, Responsibility, Resourcefulness, and Realization of the importance of achieving worthy goals and purposes.

I can remember when I was a kid we used to write the answers to questions on our fingernails. One time I got so nervous, I chewed up two years of Intermediate Algebra!

Educational theories change rapidly. We were never led to believe that life must be kind to us.

That "head-whacking" teacher told me, "If you think life must be kind to you, you are licked before you start. Don't waste your strength in being outraged because life is difficult for you. Assume that life naturally is difficult; will never be easier. Accept the inevitable and live vigorously."

Can a society that exists on instant mashed potatoes, packaged cake mixes, frozen dinners, and instant cameras teach patience to its young?

## *Birth Control*

No wonder birth control is such a problem. Look at the phrase itself--"birth control". Doesn't make sense. It's nine months before that you need the control. I'm amazed at how strong the feeling for birth control has become. You can't drive through any city or town without seeing a sign saying, "Watch Out For Children." Have you noticed how sneaky birth-control groups are getting? One of them just put out a bumper sticker: HELP STAMP OUT P.T.A.!

I'm a little suspicious of some of these birth-control pills; one of the leading side effects seems to be pregnancy. One of the birth-control pills is made of celery, peanut butter, and taffy. By the time you get finished chewing it, you're too tired.

They say that because of the oral birth-control pills, women in their sixties and seventies might still have babies. One store is adding a whole new line of maternity shawls. Frankly I think it's going to be a little embarrassing, a seventy-year-old woman giving birth--especially to a forty-year-old baby. It will challenge their husbands. I know some of these old codgers are heir-minded. Now let's see if they're heir-conditioned.

In India housewives can now dial for birth-control information. All they need to remember is two letters-NO! Do you realize what dialing for birth-control information will mean? Twenty years from now there are going to be people on this earth who owe their existence to a wrong number.

Planned Parenthood is another confusing term. It infers that kids have a choice. My wife was an expert on family planning. The day we were married, half her family moved in with us--and the other half was planning to.

I agree that sex education should begin at home but parents have such romantic ideas about telling their kids about the facts of life. It'll be spring. The mother robins will be hatching their eggs. The salmon will be fighting their way upstream. Bees will be fertilizing the little buttercups. Their kids will look up in wonderment at this eternal drama of life ever renewing itself--and *that* will be the time! You know how it actually works out? Yesterday we were in a hardware store and I heard a kid ask his dad, "What's a female plug?"

## *Business*

Business is getting better and better, according to some reports. This is particularly true for those who make a business of making reports. The business of making surveys and polls seems to have plenty of backbone, but sometimes it's lumped at the upper end. I've never been polled; I've been shafted a few times, but never polled.

Business is doubtless sound, as the experts say, but the sound is a little mournful. Probably the reason business conditions are unsettled is because so many accounts are.

Most of the so-called experts today are smart enough to tell you how to run your business and too smart to start one of their own. The most businesslike thing the government can do is to keep out of business. If business is looking up today, it's to see if taxes are coming down. The government thinks that business should be bossed by federal experts in good times and look out for itself in bad times.

New books instruct how to keep young in business. Most folks want a recipe on how to grow old in it. It seems that a number of people who went into business on the ground floor are now in the basement.

A financier says that a business slump is caused by a change in our spending habits. The change in our spending habits has been caused by a slump. The trouble with business is that it has too many prophets and not enough profits. There's no telling how good business might be if all the people studying unemployment would go to work.

Public opinion is queer. Why does it slight small business and threaten big business? What kind of business does public opinion want? The only way to bring this country unparalleled prosperity in a hurry is to let each man run another man's business for a couple of weeks. If each is as good at running the business as he is at telling how to run it, nothing could prevent us from gaining the most amazing prosperity in world history.

Most people like to give advice, and some "give until it hurts." A good scare will often help a man more than advice. Bad times have a scientific value. These are occasions a good learner does not miss.

## *Cars*

Every year Detroit tries to add something new to cars. Sometimes they add it to the engine. Sometimes they add it to the body. This year they're adding it to the price tag. The new cars are sort of a compromise. Last year's styling with next year's prices. They keep talking about crime in the streets. To me that's the price of new cars. I can remember when $150 was the down payment. Now it won't even cover the sales tax. If you want to buy a $10,000 car, it's easy. Buy a $6,000 car on time payments.

I bought a car on time and it's a fascinating experience. Our atom bombs should be as well hidden as car payment interest charges. I'm now on the 83rd month of my three-year loan--six more payments and I own the hubcaps. The car had defective brakes and I told the dealer, "I don't want you to stand behind this car--I want you to stand in front of it. I won't say how I found out this car had defective brakes, but we no longer have to back out of our garage. But in all fairness to the salesman, he didn't lie to me about the brakes. He said, "You'll love this car. There's no stopping it!" Personally, I think they ought to be sporting about it. If they can't give you brakes that work--the least they could do is give you a louder horn.

There's one new car on the market with 60 optional extras. What makes this so unusual? The motor is one of them! Sixty optional extras! Remember the good old days when a car was put together by Detroit instead of you?

You know what's fun? Combine the extras! Get a power glove compartment--everything falls out electronically.

What I like about buying a new car is all the guarantees

you get. You're guaranteed for two years--or 24,000 miles--or until something goes wrong--whichever comes first. I think every new car owner gets two shafts. One in the car and one in the warranty. Whenever anything goes wrong, they're quick to point out the Nudist Clause--all the things that aren't covered.

We're going to keep my wife's car. It's an oldie, but goodie. The car is so old the clock on the dashboard is a sun dial. But it's a wonderful car. It has two shock absorbers--me and my wife!

After looking at new models, I decided that the car in my garage isn't getting older--it's just getting bigger. Some of the new cars are so little they need a life jacket to go through a car wash. They say the big, expensive, heavy, high-powered, gas-guzzling cars are a thing of the past. For me they were never a thing of the present.

You once paid $8,000 for a car and the engine purred like a kitten. Many of today's models sound like they're clearing their throats. They're expensive. Anyone who pays sticker price for a new car can hereafter be referred to as the "stickee." If you buy one with an automatic shift you go from rich to poor in 60 seconds.

Cars have changed in the past few years. At first we were trying to save lives by installing all kinds of safety equipment. Seat belts, buzzers, air bags, shoulder harnesses; now it's more important to save gas. If you want to travel 100 miles on a gallon of gas, just set a match to it!

When it comes to safety, the automobile is only one of three principal elements involved in traffic accidents. The others are the highway and the driver. Progress in automotive safety has made a big contribution to reduction in the traffic accident rate, but it is unrealistic to pin major hope for greater traffic safety on vehicle improvements--just as it is grossly inaccurate to charge the vehicle with major responsibility for today's accident toll. Major safety gains will only come from a sound, balanced program to improve drivers and roads as well as automobiles.

## *Christmas Catalogs*

At time of year we all get bombarded with gift catalogs. If Christmas were canceled, Wisconsin would be stuck with three million tons of cheese. Look at these catalogs: they're loaded with fruit cakes, candies, seven-layer cakes, and chocolate clusters. Just from turning the pages my thumb gained seven pounds. One outfit is selling chocolate-covered pickles for Christmas. That's a great idea. Now you can have morning sickness before you are pregnant.

Everybody seems to specialize. One outfit sells nothing but cheese. Another has hams. Another has salamis. Another has chocolates. In January there's a company that really cleans up. They sell monogrammed Rolaids.

Thanks to these holiday fruit cakes, people are suffering from a new stomach ailment--crushed ulcers. A lot of these cakes come from Germany, and mark my word--Hitler is alive and mixing batter. Someone gave me one of those fruit cakes, and I don't know if it's for Christmas or revenge. I think the ingredients are brandy, fruit, nuts, and cement.

Christmas is when they sell 80 million dollars worth of those gorgeous gourmet food packages. Inside there's six bucks worth of food. You're paying for cardboard, stuffing, and ribbons. Now I know what they mean by gift-rapped. And the prices--$49.50, $69.50, $89.50. They're like CARE packages for J. Paul Getty!

One catalog offers a traditional American Christmas. The tree comes from Canada; the ornaments come from Hong Kong; the lights come from Japan; and the idea comes from Bethlehem. They offer lavender ornaments;

crimson tinsel; puce lights. I would have bought them, but I was afraid the tree would throw up.

Catalog shopping may be fine, but I prefer the hustle and bustle in the stores. It's unbelievable. You don't walk-- you're just carried along with the crowd. I turned to one woman and said, "Have you ever seen such confusion?" She said, "You oughta know. This is the ladies' room!"

## *Christmas Shopping*

Christmas is such an exciting time. Kids are asking for toys and games and bikes and Santa Claus is saying, "Ho! Ho! Ho!" Fathers are looking at the price tags and saying, "How? How? How?"

We love to go to the mall just to watch the little kids visit with Santa. Whoever said, "Talk is cheap," never listened to a kid tell Santa what he wants for Christmas.

The little tykes are always curious how Santa can get into their homes--especially if they don't have a fireplace. One department store Santa Claus tells them, "through a hole in your daddy's pocket!"

One department store Santa Claus showed up drunk, which was awkward. But what really made it embarrassing, the first little girl went back to her mother and said, "Guess what? Santa uses the same mouthwash as Daddy!"

Another department store Santa told me he suffers from water on the knee--sometimes six or seven times a day. This Santa is experienced. He said, "Sometimes I get the feeling the Santa Claus story is dying a little each year. You tell it to a seven-year-old today and right away he wants to know how many pounds of thrust the sleigh develops before it leaves the launching pad. You start with Dancer and Prancer after that."

Fathers rise to great heights during the Christmas season. A father and his little daughter stood in front of the shopping center Santa Claus. The father said, "Yes, Virginia, this is Santa Claus--and that was Santa Claus at K-Mart, and at Ward's, at Penney's, and that was Santa Claus on the street corner." His little daughter said, "How can there be so many Santa Clauses?" The father turned to the fella in the big red suit and said, "Tell Virginia how you fell into the Xerox machine!"

One little youngster told Santa he was disappointed in what he got last year and asked, "Do you have malpractice insurance?" Christmas is the time kids and money both sprout wings.

Kids are shrewd today. They go up to the department store Santa Claus and tell him everything they want for Christmas in a voice loud enough for Grandma to hear. Christmas is a very fair season. There are kids who no longer believe in Santa Claus and there are department store Santa Clauses who no longer believe in kids. One kid looked up at Santa Claus and said, "Are you a politician?" Santa said, "Of course not. Why would you think I'm a politician?" The kid said, " 'Cause you always promise more than you deliver."

It isn't easy being a department store Santa Claus. You spend eight hours lifting kids onto your lap and you'd swear the last one was wearing lead shorts. In fact, December 26th is when department store Santa Clauses all over the country go out and have their laps resoled.

All the kids ask for dolls and toys and there's a jillion different kinds of dolls and toys. Frankly, I could never understand why certain dolls are so popular. You know the ones I mean. They cry from either end--and cost you $40

All you get for it is a kidney problem. One is called a Neurotic Doll. It's wound up already. Then there's a teenage doll that's so realistic, it doesn't walk--it slouches. And there are complete wardrobes for dolls. I wanted to buy a wedding gown for one of those dolls--$30! I didn't buy it. Let her sneak off to motels. They have one doll that does nothing but cry. I think it got a look at its price tag.

All the toys this Christmas are electronic--robots, rockets, walkie-talkies, space stations. For those of you who want to give the ideal after-Christmas gift--two dozen batteries. Years ago, your biggest problem on a cold Christmas morning was getting the car started. Now it's getting the toys started. When I was a kid the power to operate toys came from kids. Because of batteries kids don't play with toys any more. They observe them! They watch them do all the things the kids would be doing if they didn't have the toy in the first place. Thanks to batteries, you never have to worry about a kid getting a broken leg, or a fractured wrist, or a bruised knee any more. Electrocuted, yes!

Nowadays, the problem isn't keeping up with the Joneses. It's keeping up with their kids.

## Christmas Trees

Something's gotta be done about the price of Christmas trees. I paid $35 for one and I brought it home in the car. Not in the trunk--the glove compartment. My wife could wear it for a corsage. Where do they get all these pygmy trees? It's like a whole forest went on Slimfast. They say only God can make a tree and sometimes I wish He would retail it too. Discount! That's the magic word these days. I bought my tree at a place selling discount Christmas trees--as if God put a list price on them.

I know what I'll find under our tree Christmas morning--7000 needles, and then we'll spend a quiet day taking down the tree. Actually we'll be taking down the branches. The needles came down last week. It's kinda sad to see something so stately, standing there with bare limbs and just a few bits of tinsel clinging to it. That's why I never liked burlesque.

They sell artificial trees, but those silver, celluloid branches don't make it for me; it's like we're celebrating the birth of Dupont. I know those artificial trees are full, uniform, and flameproof--but I've yet to see anybody go up to one, take a deep breath, and say, "Mmmm, smell that plastic!" Looking at all these vinyl Christmas trees with the full, balanced branches--the perfectly tapered silhouette--the non-shed needles--I wonder if God ever feels inadequate?

Did you know that most of the mistletoe you see around these days is plastic? I didn't until this year when I stood under a sprig and had an uncontrollable desire to kiss a transistor radio.

Things were so much simpler in the old days. They could do things like deck the halls with boughs of holly. I gotta get permission just to put up a calendar. In the old days, they did wild things for Christmas. Like they brought home a yule log and it stayed lit for twelve days. Today, the only thing that stays lit for twelve days is my brother-in-law.

# *College*

Our neighbors are applying for an extension of their son's college loan. They had the board, room, and tuition figured out, but they didn't count on bail. Their son's college education is already showing tangible value. For one thing, it has cured his mother of bragging about him.

Sending a youngster to college educates parents. It teaches them how to do without things.

Lots of kids can't read today and that's bad. The U.S. cannot exist without readers and writers. The country could neither carry on work nor transmit knowledge, and the civilization would grind to a halt.

Ours is a government of the many, not the few, and it is based on trust in its citizens. It trusts them to have formed the habit of finding out, and that means the habit of reading. We cannot afford a nations of non-readers, of lazy minds and the boredom that comes from knowing little and caring less.

At least today's report cards prove that kids aren't taking mind-expanding drugs. The main reason for education is to learn how to think, and we're failing there.

Lions are never caught in mouse traps. To catch lions you must think in terms of lions, not in terms of mice. Our minds are always creating traps of one kind or another and what we catch depends on the thinking we do. It is our thinking that attracts what we receive--and we learn to think by reading!

We're putting our future into the hands of our children-- but how will our country absorb all these baton twirlers?

## Condoms And Compassion

I know a gas station owner who thinks it's funny to keep a prophylactic dispenser on the wall of his women's restroom. However, he never puts condoms in the machine.

"I get money out of that machine every week, but I never get any complaints from the women," he says.

That gas station owner had better circle his wagons. Some day "she" will come. "She" will be wearing lipstick up to her nose and her hair will look like she just flunked electrician school. "She" will be so ugly she has to tie a pork chop around her neck to get the pit bull to come. "She" will not complain. "She" will perform surgery in that women's rest room--with a chain saw.

There are a lot of inconsiderate people in the world today. They lack compassion for their fellowmen.

We have some young neighbors. The other evening when he came home from work he found her sitting on the floor in the kitchen, holding a razor blade ready to cut her wrists. I just can't figure that out. She had the whole damn day to kill herself--why did she wait until he came home? That doesn't reflect much compassion or consideration.

I guess she was getting bored. He told me she would rather watch *Hee Haw* than make love. She would say, "...not now, honey, the horse is about to talk."

Today everybody has sex on their minds. When you reach my age that's the only place you have it. Sex education has had a lot to do with today's attitudes. One thing about sex education in schools is kids still cannot add or subtract, but they sure know how to multiply. And they're all worried about safe sex. One kid said he called a sex telephone number and suffered an ear infection. He's suing the phone company.

Things are different today. When I went to the home of the first girl I dated, my sex education began when her father opened the door. He had a dog the size of a piano, and he began reading me my rights. "What time will you bring her home? Where are you going? There will be no speeding, parking, or drinking. Do you have a full tank of gas? Let me see your driver's license."

I finally said, "To hell with the girl. How much do you want for that dog?"

## Cost Of Living

Everybody has something witty to say about money. For example, they say you can't take it with you. True enough, but these days where can you go without it? Some people say money will not make you happy. This may be true, but it sure puts your creditors in a better frame of mind. Money may not buy friends, but it certainly gives you a better class of enemies!

The government deplores the fact that the outgo of 28 percent of American families exceeds their income. Look who's talking! The trouble with many elected politicians is that they think what they got from the public last November was not a mandate but a charge-a-plate.

I never worry about what's happening on the New York Stock Exchange or on the American Stock Exchange because I have all my money in over-the-counter invest-ments--groceries!

The increased cost of living may simply be the price we have to pay for changing standards of living. The grocery manufacturers contend that one-third of all food store sales are products that did not exist ten years ago.

Living costs no more than it used to, if you live as people used to. If people were willing to buy the same foods they bought before World War II, packaged the same way as they were packaged then, their food bills would take only an estimated 16 percent of their disposable income instead of the estimated 25 percent now spent.

Here's one that will shock you, "Live beyond your income and you'll age before your time." According to studies made by three universities, people who have learned to live within their means live longer and retain mental and physical alertness for a longer time than those who habitually spend more than they earn.

If that's true, we're all in the same boat--the Titanic!

## *Crime*

Thanks to Supreme Court decisions, making an arrest these days is like cooking with teflon. It's hard to make anything stick. For the first time in history, even the churches are locked up. If you want to go in and pray, you have to go up to the door, knock three times, and say, "Peter sent me!"

More violence is directed at police. Thirty years ago it was hard to find an unmarked cop's car. Nowadays it's hard to find an unmarked cop.

They say that crime doesn't pay--except for publishers and TV executives. Today, amid hard times, crime is doing handsomely. The television networks plan a bumper crop of crime dramas for the fall. Book stores specializing in crime stories say business is better than ever. One media analyst bluntly states, "In hard times, there is a certain amount of daydreaming going on. People wish they could pull a bank job and get away with it and that affects their choice of literature, their television watching, and their movie- going." The most popular TV shows are those with the most violence.

These are jaded, cynical times. When secretaries work late they can't go home by themselves. I know a girl who carries a whistle, but even that isn't perfect. Last night she had her purse snatched, and as the thief was running away, she blew this whistle like mad--and within thirty seconds, you know what happened? She got a cab.

People become insensitive to the real horrors of this earth when they see horror pictures over and over again. On March 30, 1981, America watched in horror as President Reagan was shot by a would-be assassin. Television viewers saw that incident over and over again until it became just another blob of news footage.

I had a terrible dream. The President went on television and declared that he had been advised on reliable scientific authority that the world would come to an end at midnight-- and nobody heard him because they were watching the latest science-fiction horror movie!

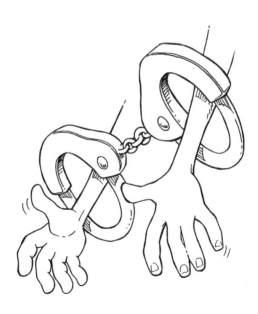

Statistics indicate that juries are hung more frequently than murderers. One reason there are so many murders committed in this country is because the murderers seldom are. Everybody seems to speak with conviction on the subject of crime except some of our juries. Under the laws of this country, a man is innocent until he is proved guilty. Then if he isn't insane he is pardoned. The real crime wave is the failure of juries to convict.

It is just as well justice is blind; she might not like some of the things done in her name if she could see them. It is amazing how we lock up the witnesses and let the prisoner out on bail. With all of the "bleeding hearts" looking after the welfare of criminals, it is possible for a man to murder both his parents and then plead for mercy on the grounds that he is an orphan.

What would happen to this country if all its citizens had no higher conception of freedom than the right to get drunk? It is a man's inalienable right to make a fool of himself, but he should not use up all his privileges.

## *Dieting*

America seems to have become the sandwich capital of the world. Any way you slice it Americans eat a lot of bread; an average of 70 pounds each annually, and that's a lot of dough.

Maybe that's why we're hearing so much about diets-- diet pills, diet exercises, and computerized calorie counters. There are all kinds of diets. There's a diet that guarantees you'll lose two pounds a week. It's called the Impacted Molar Diet. I know a woman who just went on a foolproof diet. She can only eat when the news is good!

I went on the Drinking Man's Diet and it's great. I lost six pounds and three weekends. Some people call it the Drinking Man's Diet. Some call it the Air Force Diet. Either way you wind up flying. According to the Drinking Man's Diet, anything loaded with alcohol and fat is okay. They even have a Dieters Cocktail. Three of them and you look thin and talk thick. If this idea works, we'll end up with 190-million skinny drunks.

I'll admit I'm a little overweight. It all started the day my rowing machine sank. I won't even weigh myself on the bathroom scale until after I shave. Now I'm on Pepsi and oysters--that's for us who think young and feel old.

They say that when you go on a diet, the first thing you lose is your temper. I don't know about that. My wife went to a diet doctor and the first thing she lost was $300. Dietetic foods are so expensive you have to lose weight. There's no money left over for cake.

I know a fellow who had a medical checkup and the doctor said he had to give up wine, sex, and song. The guy turned pale. He said, "Doc, I can't! I'd starve to death!" The doctor said, "You'd starve to death by giving up wine, sex, and song? What do you do?" He said, "I sing dirty drinking songs."

You know what bugs me? All these doctors saying you should give up smoking, drinking, overeating, and going out with fast women. As far as I can see, it doesn't do you a bit of good, but you die much healthier.

It's heartrending to see the members of a diet club who fall off the wagon. One member showed up under the influence of chocolate cream pie--another O.D.'d on Twinkies. Fat? If they wanted to let it all hang out, it would take two trips.

My doctor told me it was disgraceful the way I abused my body by overeating. At least, I think that's what he said.

With his smoker's cough, it's hard to understand him.

I'm not fat. It's just that my body built up a natural immunity to being thin. But we're trying a little diet where anything that tastes out-and-out good is out! Our neighbor lost 22 pounds and it's all because of the grapefruit diet. Every morning he goes down to the market and unloads 800 crates of grapefruit.

To most people, the theory that heart disease comes from fat food is much less palatable than the older and more familiar explanation that it is the price of success in a high tension world. A British physician put it bluntly writing in the *British Medical Journal*, "How much nicer it is, when stricken with a coronary thrombosis, to be told it is due to gluttony and physical indolence."

Today everybody seems to be on some sort of health kick. One thing bothers me. If money can't buy health, why is health food so expensive? And the world is flooded with advice. For years people kept telling me to "smell the flowers along the way." So I did, and now I have hay fever!

As you grow older you learn to accept the impossible, do without the indispensable and bear the intolerable. I am a person completely in tune with the spirit, the philosophy, the tempo of our time. Other than that, I feel pretty good.

## *Don't Ask Grandpa!*

Grandfathers can handle the funny questions asked by cute toddlers: "Why is the sky blue? Why do they call them lady bugs? Where do the stars go in the daytime?" All basic stuff.

But when those cute little toddlers grow up, have kids of their own, and you have great grandchildren, the ball game has a new set of rules. Instead of the great grandchildren asking questions you soon learn that the adult toddlers are still seeking the wisdom of the years from grandpa. Questions asked by young adults are different and dangerous.

The best way to put a stop to this modern questioning is with modern answers. Here are a few guaranteed "Don't ask me" answers:

*Question:* "Don't you think little Sammy has a lot of potential--isn't he a smart kid?"

*Answer:* "He sure is. He reminds me of your dad. When he was nine we thought we had a Nobel prize-winner. But when he was 29, we said, 'At least he doesn't steal.'"

*Question:* We've been having a little discipline problem with Jimmy. How did your mother discipline you?"

*Answer:* "I was a cesarean baby. Every time I misbehaved I had to look at mother's scar."

*Question:* "Did you have sex education when you were a kid?"

*Answer:* "No. Every time I asked what the boy dog and girl dog were doing in the yard, I was told they were dancing. I didn't know the difference until I went to the Junior-Senior Prom. I was suspended from school."

*Question:* "Did you have baby-sitters when you were a kid?"

*Answer:* "Mine was a real 'pro'. She fed me applesauce with a caulking gun. First time I was ever fed through the nose."

*Question:* "Marie and I have tried and tried to have a baby with no success. What should we do?"

*Answer:* "Don't worry about it. Hell, if you're going to be a failure at something, that's as much fun as anything else."

*Question:* "Did you have any trouble coping with being the youngest one in the family?"

*Answer:* "Not at all. The folks simply told me ...Here are

the car keys. There's the liquor cabinet. Do what you have to do. We're tired."

*Question:* "They say smoking marijuana destroys your night vision. Do you believe that?"

*Answer:* "That might explain some of the people you've been waking up with."

*Question:* "Do you know where we can get a really good deal on a microwave?"

*Answer:* "You'll have to ask Grandma. She's the Bargain Queen. She bought a microwave oven for 50% off. It has a cracked glass in the window, but it works real well. Of course, the cat lost all of its hair, but who needs a cat?"

*Question:* "I have an upset stomach. Is there some kind of a bug going around?"

*Answer:* "Yes, there's a bug. My cousin had that and he's been brain dead for a week."

*Question:* "What do you think we should give Sonny for his graduation present?"

*Answer:* "Luggage--fully packed. Tell him there's a great big beautiful world out there and he should hit the road and check it out."

*Question:* "Jack and Jill have been married 10 years. Now they've started having babies. Why are they doing that?"

*Answer:* "They took out a mortgage on their house. It happens every time. Just take out a mortgage and here they come, bam! bam! bam!"

*Question:* "How do you feel about women carrying guns to protect themselves?"

*Answer:* "Women carrying guns smell like they're wearing perfume put out by the National Rifle Association."

*Question:* "Have you seen Sonny driving that new car we gave him?"

*Answer:* "Yeah, that's really neat. I especially like the way his plastic Jesus hangs onto the dice when he takes a curve."

*Question:* "Are we playing the stereo too loud for you,

Grandpa?"

*Answer:* "I don't think so. It just rearranged my liver spots. I guess I needed that."

Answers such as these discourage arguments when the "grand young adults" come to visit. They quickly learn the old man has the home court advantage!

## *Economizing*

Remember when we put electricity in our house because it was clean? Now we're cleaned because we put electricity in the house--and the phone company also better be careful about raising the rates. There are very few conversations worth the money now, and can you imagine paying $.32 just to mail a letter? Nowadays, who has news that good?

A lot of people are finding that even two jobs aren't enough. There's even a song about it, "I Was Failing Along on Moonlight Pay." Everything keeps going up. We used to have 5 and 10s. Now we have 7-11s.

I can't help being depressed. I just realized it's costing me more to insure my car than my life. I've learned you only need one thing to buy an economy car--a luxury salary. Be honest now. Did you ever expect to pay $18,000 for anything that didn't come with a lawn?

A lot of people are worrying how to keep the wolf from the door; others are figuring out how they can throw it out of the house before it has pups. We've noticed that often when a family is fighting to keep the wolf away from the door, the stork takes the opportunity to slip down the chimney.

Blessed are the poor for they'll never be shown up in biographies, and they can put on a cheap shirt without having to pull out thirty-two pins.

Just pretending to be rich keeps some people poor. We try to keep up with the Joneses, and they never seem to make a pit stop.

Early habits set a pattern for the way we run our lives. Most of us are like the fellow whose mother, when he was a baby, hired a nurse to wheel him about in his carriage. And he has been pushed for money ever since! Most of us are pushed for money all through our lives, and the more we earn, the higher our living standard and the harder we are pushed. I guess a man never realizes the blessing of being poor, 'til he gets over it. "It is a great thing to come from a state of poverty," says an industrial magnate. It is great when you come far enough from it.

They're telling us to economize, but economizing is always a very delicate matter. Like the fella who does circumcisions, you have to be very careful what you cut.

## *Education*

The nation's educational system is under fire these days. It seems modern education has greatly simplified the three R's--from reading, 'riting, and 'rithmetic to rah, rah, rah. Nowadays a student picks up geography from a steering wheel; arithmetic from a touch tone phone; and the alphabet from the radio call list.

Raising kids is a peculiar business. You spend half your time trying to instill them with knowledge, and the other half telling them not to be so damn smart. Maybe they have it too easy. My grandson wanted a $50 pocket calculator for his math homework. I said, "I'll give you something even better. It adds, subtracts, multiplies, divides, corrects its own mistakes, and doesn't require batteries. He said, "What's it called?" I said, "A pencil."

They say we've raised a generation of "functional illiterates." According to the Literacy Volunteers of America, a nonprofit group headquartered in Syracuse, N.Y., 23 million adults in this country--one in five--cannot decipher an ordinary bus, train or airline schedule, cannot understand the explanation of a finance charge or an installment contract--can't even address a letter so it arrives at its proper destination! LVA says this is costing the U.S. $6 billion per year in welfare and unemployment payments.

According to an educator, illiterate children are much harder to manage. They can't mind their Ps and Qs if they don't know their ABCs.

Today's youngsters have learned that it's far easier to sit passively as a member of the TV audience than it is to master reading the English language. That's why they like the "look-say" method of reading. Look-say is learning by pictures--and if you don't think you can learn by pictures, you've never seen *Playboy*. I won't say how the look-say method has worked out, but on college campuses across America remedial reading is more popular than making out.

One of the drawbacks of the look-say method is that every time a kid sees a typographical error, he thinks it's a new word--and when it comes to abbreviations, forget it!

How will 23 million functional illiterates help their kids with their homework?

They say today's kids have a problem with writing. A lot of adults aren't doing so red hot either--here are some samples of poor grammar, sentences taken from actual letters received by the welfare department in applications for support:

"I am writing the welfare department to say that my baby was born two years old. When do I get my money?"

"Mrs. Jones has not had any clothes for a year and has been visited regularly by the clergy."

"I cannot get sick pay. I have six children. Can you tell me why?"

"This is my eighth child. What are you going to do about it?"

"Please find out for certain if my husband is dead. The man I am now living with can't eat or do anything until he knows."

"I am very much annoyed to find you have branded my son illiterate. This is a dirty lie as I was married a week before he was born."

"In answer to your letter, I have given birth to a boy weighing ten pounds. I hope this is satisfactory."

"I am forwarding my marriage certificate and three children, one of which is a mistake as you can see."

"Unless I get my husband's money pretty soon, I will be forced to live an immortal life."

"You have changed my little boy to a girl. Will this make any difference?"

"I have no children as yet as my husband is a truck driver and works day and night."

"In accordance with your instructions I have given birth to twins in the enclosed envelope."

"I want my money as quick as I can get it. I've been in bed with the doctor for two weeks and he doesn't do me any good. If things don't improve, I will have to send for another doctor."

## *Elections*

Religion has always been a part of politics. For years, voters have looked at some of the candidates and said, "Good Lord!" Remember when X indicated an unknown quantity? It still does when put on a ballot. We should all be grateful for elections. They're our Preparation H for the seat of government.

There's a reason why Congressional elections are held in years that are even. It gives voters a chance to get likewise. We've learned that a political platform is like the second stanza of the Star Spangled Banner. Everybody knows it's there, but very few remember the words.

Congressmen are firm believers in the buddy system. You ask any of them if they were in favor of the pay raise and they say, "Not me, Buddy."

Congressmen are now earning more than $130,000 a year. It's ridiculous. I know doctors who don't make that much in a month. The President wants to put a lid on increases in hospital costs and in all fairness, the hospitals are taking it rather well. To show there's no hard feelings, the next time a member of the Administration goes into a Washington hospital, there will be a special piece of equipment in which to keep the bed pan--it's called a refrigerator.

The cost of running Congress may be small potatoes, but the gravy is something else. The problem is government isn't so much non-essential spending as non-essential spenders. Abraham Lincoln will be remembered for many things, but foremost among them is this: He proved that it really is possible for a poor boy to become a politician--and remain poor.

We have elections to correct our mistakes. Democracy

does not mean the silly belief that the majority of the people are always right in any given decision. It does mean the passionate belief that the people have the right to be wrong. They have the capacity to correct their mistakes and amend their excesses, in a free and generous spirit which no other form of government can afford. Today we are busy correcting a lot of past mistakes.

The secrecy of the voting booth gives all Americans the opportunity to choose their leaders, to exercise their rights and to check their zippers.

# *Exercise*

Exercise and diet are the "in" things today. Everybody you talk to is either out of breath or burping. If it weren't for coughing, I'd get no exercise at all. To me up, down--up, down--is reading the stock market page.

So many people now run 10 miles a day, it could create a problem. Not enough heart attacks to go around. I have only one thing to say about runners: Anyone who says they run 10 miles a day with their muscles aching, their hearts pounding, and their lungs on fire--because it makes them feel good--will also lie about other things.

Running 10 miles a day isn't as simple as it looks. Your feet have to control your stride; your feet have to control your balance; your feet have to control your thrust. One might even go so far as to say, if you do run 10 miles a day you've gotta have your brains in your feet.

And running is great if you're overweight. You don't lose any pounds, but if you run 10 miles on a hot day, people stand so far away you look thin.

The statistics tell the story. They show that every year there are a few million more runners while the birth rate is declining. Which can mean only one thing: For the first time in history, more Americans are interested in running than in catching.

Runners are perfectionists. They won't do anything unless they have the right equipment. I know a runner who dropped dead. It's the first time I ever saw an Adidas coffin.

A practical runner is one who always carries three phone numbers--for a doctor, for a hospital, and for a taxi. Some try to get their exercise by pushing away from the dining table. It is very discouraging. My wife is on a diet, I'm on a diet, the dog's on a diet. But the only thing that is losing weight is the refrigerator. You can always tell a person who's just given up a diet. They go out to the kitchen for a snack and put something on a low-fat cracker--a pork chop.

You know you've overdone your diet if you're standing by a curb, a car pulls up, parks, the driver gets out and tries to put a nickel in your ear.

# *February*

February is an interesting month; there's Ground Hog Day, Lincoln's Birthday, Valentine's Day, and two birthdays for George Washington. Old George gets two shots at being memorialized, a holiday and a "traditional" day. Honest Abe and the Ground Hog seem to be in the same category as St. Valentine.

The Ground Hog always sees his shadow, and that scares hell out of folks in the Eastern states. They've already worn out three pairs of rubber boots and one pair of shoes and they dread six more weeks when their noses run and their cars won't.

Then comes Valentine's Day. The stores started selling those big, heart-shaped boxes of candy before Santa went up the chimney. I like those candy boxes where you have to read a map to find the good ones. You can get eye strain and tooth decay at the same time. True love is giving your wife a five-pound heart of chocolates--and your favorite is peanut brittle. Flowers are also very big on Valentine's Day. I'm giving my wife a dozen roses to match the color I see the most in her hair. It's called, "hair-roller pink."

But George Washington really steals the February show. On the 21st we have a legal holiday; some folks get a "day off," followed by an "off day" the 22nd. George was the one with wooden false teeth. When he took the toothpaste test he had 21 percent fewer knotholes.

Every Washington's Birthday, all the bakeries have layer cakes with a little hatchet on top. Which is fine--but they're not cherry cakes--they're chocolate cakes. We're growing a whole generation of kids who think Washington chopped down the Hershey plant!

Remember the picture of Washington crossing the Delaware? People keep asking why George was standing up in the boat. He had to stand up. Every time he sat down, someone handed him an oar.

All over the East there signs reading: "George Washington Slept Here"--"George Washington Slept Here." If you think the British were worried about George, you should have seen Martha.

## Flu Fight

Nowadays you don't have to worry about things like colds. You can take pills to eliminate nasal congestion, pills to counteract the symptoms of sore throat, coughs, and headaches; pills to give you quick energy and increase your body tone and vigor. Thanks to medical science, people are dying every day who never looked better.

The way I see it--a miracle drug is anything that'll do 25 percent of the things the label says it will. I'm unlucky. Last week I got a cold, so I took the stuff that opens the nasal passages. While they were open I caught another cold. My nose did more running than a tourist in Mexico.

A lot of people are suffering from the Hong Kong flu. Everybody is saying, "Ah Chou!" The government is going to do something to prevent a flu epidemic. Starting Monday, it's illegal to exhale. These colds are spreading throughout the country. Yesterday I had cereal for breakfast and it was going, "Snap! Crackle! Sniff!"

Not long ago, before antibiotics, everyone was given a

shot of penicillin administered in the rump. One year I got so many penicillin shots I sent my red flannels to the tailor to have the flap taken out and a bulls-eye put in. I looked like a junkie with a terrible aim. My doctor did nothing but give penicillin shots for five straight days--then he went beserk! He said, "I can't take it any more! It's like being a midget in a nudist parade!"

We've been able to put a man on the moon, but we still haven't found a cure for the common cold. Doesn't it bother you a little to realize we're spending $10,000,000 for preventive medicine, but $100,000,000 for get-well cards? Scientists are now on the brink of making one of the greatest medical discoveries of all time--fluoridated chicken soup!

Scientists brag about organ transplants, artificial insemination, and all the time they're wearing masks. If something goes wrong, you don't even know who to blame. But they'll tell you, "There's only one way to avoid the sniffles. Drink lots of water. Lots of water! Let's face it--when have you ever seen a fish with a cold?

## Food Prices

Meat is so scarce in our neighborhood that anyone who has a grease fire is bragging. Meat is now being reserved for special occasions. I went to a birthday party and it was the first time I saw a hamburger with candles.

There's nothing complicated about the meat-packing business. Ranchers sell beef by the head; middlemen sell it by the side; and consumers get it in the end.

Seafood is so high if you find a pearl you break even, and salmon is so expensive they no longer swim upstream to spawn--they take a cab.

The price of lettuce is making some strange scenes in restaurants. The other night we saw a guy toss a salad with a safety net. I won't say what they charged for a chicken dinner, but it's the last time I'm going to pay an arm and a leg for a wing and a breast. One customer asked the waiter to put a steak on his credit card--and it fit!

I'm always worried by those fancy places where the waiters wear gloves. You can't help but wonder what's in the food they're afraid to touch. It reminds me of a restaurant that was so bad the cook wouldn't even lick his fingers. And I always get a little uncomfortable at a buffet dinner. Maybe it's the armed guard around the roast beef.

Eating out is fun, but I'm always suspicious of any Chinese dinner that starts off with One Tum soup. Whenever I look at a menu and find Stroganoff I can't help but wonder if he was a fellow who complained a lot.

We went to the opening of a very exclusive drive-in restaurant. You order Gatorade and they ask you what year. They have two specialties: Poulet a la Ferrari--that's a chicken that has been run over by a sports car. Poulet a la Chevrolet costs half as much; that bird was hit by a pick-up truck. They even have a fortune teller who reads the bubbles in Schlitz. Another fortune teller reads the grease on napkins and they have Kaopectate on the wine list.

Last Sunday we had a fantastic meal. A neighbor down the block invited the entire neighborhood over for a barbecue. It just shows what can happen when a person's heart opens up and his freezer breaks down.

# *Football*

Fall is the time of year when Saturday afternoons are devoted to contact sports--college football and getting out of the stadium parking lot. Football season is the one time of year when you can walk down the street with a blanket on one arm and a girl on the other and not have any people asking silly questions.

One of the hardiest creatures around is the college football fan. In him are combined qualities of indestructibility: the stamina of an Olympic champion and the nerves of Matt Dillon.

These hardy folk prove their mettle each Saturday by flocking in ever-increasing numbers to the many cavernous, concrete bowls scattered around the country. Their love for the game, the color, and massive "togetherness" is such that a few mild discomforts count for nothing.

Take the trip to the stadium, for example. We've found that it really isn't so bad. It might even be thought of as a challenge. After all, it takes skill to maneuver a vehicle in open competition with several thousand other vehicles all bent on the same purpose: to find a parking place within three miles of the stadium.

After skipping five or six blocks at a pretty good clip, and a little hike up the ramp (laughingly known as "Coronary Climbosis"), we reach our seats on the 65th row. At last we're comfortably wedged into our seats, our hearts pumping strongly from anticipation of the kickoff and good, healthy over-exertion.

From our vantage point, the players resemble microbes wriggling under a microscope. But we have little trouble following the action, because two or three of our neighbors have radios tuned into the game--plus several other games around the country.

We also enjoy the quaint ritual known as, "Pass these down, will you, buddy?" Someone in the middle of the row shouts an order for a half-dozen cokes and all of us in between form a sort of water brigade passing the cups from person to person. Payment comes down the line and soon the change comes back. It gives a feeling of participation.

Football is a great sport. What other game has 12 gorgeous pompom girls standing on the sidelines. Who do the players pat on the fanny? Each other!

## *Fund Raising*

At fund-raising banquets you get service with a smile. The waiters can't get over what you're paying for that food. Have you ever gone to a $100-a-plate dinner? No matter how worthy the cause, it's an eerie feeling to drop a french fry and think, "There goes five bucks."

Isn't it wonderful the way politicians try to add that warm, personal touch? Yesterday I got a fund-raising letter addressed, To Whom It May Concern. It said, "Dear Whom: As you know, this is a $1,000-a-plate dinner." I don't know who came up with that price, but I think it's my dentist. I didn't really think they were going to charge $1,000 a plate until I saw the finance chairman and the treasurer wearing nylon stockings--over their heads!

The latest concept in fund raising is the benefit cocktail party. It gives you a chance to raise funds and hell at the same time. I understand that the biggest pledges were signed with swizzle sticks.

In a more direct method of fund-raising, the finance chairman says, "Each member in favor of our meeting the budget this year, please raise your hand--and have a $500 check in it!" An amateur fund-raiser says, "Give till it hurts." So does a professional fund-raiser, only he applies a little novocaine first.

It's discouraging to belong to an organization that's always raising money. You're never sure whether you're one of the flock or one of the fleeced, especially when the fund-raiser is called Chairman of the Shearing Committee.

A politician was getting dressed to go to a fund-raising dinner when his wife exploded. She said, "It's ridiculous. Every night it's either a meeting, a reception, a banquet or a testimonial. I think I'd drop dead on the spot if ever you spent an evening at home." He said, "Please dear. Under the new rules we're not allowed to accept bribes."

Oh yes--regarding the $1,000-a-plate invitation--I told them I couldn't throw my money around like that. I've got the government to support.

## Gardening

Each March the seed catalogs arrive and you get carried away with ambition, enthusiasm, and peat moss. It's the pictures that do it. There are magnificent four-color reproductions of roses, chrysanthemums and marigolds.

The first sign of the mature, knowledgeable gardener is the realization that whatever he does, whatever he buys, whatever he grows will look nothing like those pictures. Personally, I think they're all posed by professional flowers at $50 an hour.

Some of the captions under the pictures get pretty exotic. One catalog described a particular type of violet as: "Not much in beds but grows wild in the woods." I didn't know if I was reading *Burpee* or *Playboy*.

And they're always cross-pollinating and changing and improving the flowers--as if God needed help. The big triumph this year is an odorless, thornless rose that lasts for months. I saw one and it's really remarkable. You can't tell it from plastic.

But the seeds, bulbs, and plants are really the smallest part of gardening. The biggest part is blisters. You spend three hours on a Saturday planting tulips, and your knees look like they're blowing bubble gum. Gardening brings almost as many people to their knees as religion--only the words they use are a little different. The trouble with having a green thumb is that it's often accompanied by a red face and purple knees.

There's some good science fiction in today's seed advertisements. The Jolly Red Giant is advertising a six-pound tomato--one slice makes a plateful--two slices make a pound! So big it takes two hands to hold them! They don't say how big a tree it takes to produce these giants. I can't see a 20-foot high tomato tree in my back yard producing these blood-shot grapefruit.

I have enough trouble with sick trees without adding a tomato tree to my list of patients. I have a spruce on the critical list. Our tree doctor has a real trunkside manner--he stands there, holding a branch and looking at his watch. Then turns and utters those dreaded words, "Dry rot!" You want to know what can save it? Money!

## *Generic Shopping*

Shopping--not baseball--is our national sport. Many people buy things they never dreamed they needed. They go to stores the way Izaak Walton would approach a trout stream, full of the sense of excitement and competence.

Excitement has become the key ingredient of all advertising and selling. We pick up this excitement in our homes through TV, magazines, and newspapers, and we carry this excitement to the store.

Did you ever see anything so bland as the generic shelves in the supermarket? Everything looks alike--all white cans and black labels. It's as exciting as watching them change the water in the gold fish tanks.

A lot of people are confused about the difference between generic and brand names, but it's simple. A generic name would be Vitamin E. The brand name would be Honeymoon Helper.

One of the most successful packaging techniques, experts say, involves using colors that appeal to a shopper's psychological needs. We know that red is an impulse color, an action color. Red--especially when it's used in packaging--catches the eye and causes emotional response. The whole world is familiar with Coca-Cola's red label, red can, and red vending machines. Campbell's soups have red labels to indicate they're "full strength."

Maybe if they put a Coke machine in the generic brand section it would generate some enthusiasm. Watch the faces of shoppers wending their way through the great White Valley of No-Name brands--they are bewildered, their eyes seemingly searching for a long-lost friend.

A ton of money is spent choosing product names which fit the shopper's subconscious conception of why she, or he, needs the product. The person who worries a lot about perspiration odor or stains will respond positively to deodorant names like Ban or Veto--the white package with black words "Deodorant Spray" has about the same sales appeal as an ash tray for a motorcycle.

## Gobbledygook

Because the U.S. economy is in a period of "negative growth," people in Washington are suggesting there may be a need for "revenue enhancement" measures.

That means the business slump may make it necessary to raise taxes.

Negative growth and revenue enhancement may not sound alarming because they weren't meant to. They are classic examples of euphemisms used by government officials who don't want to tell it the way it is in plain English.

If you're going to work with government today, you must understand government office vocabulary. Here are a few examples:

"It is in process." Hopelessly wrapped up in red tape.

"We will look into it." By the time the wheel makes a full turn, we assume you have forgotten about it, too.

"A program." Any assignment that can't be completed by one telephone call.

"Expedite." To confound confusion with commotion.

"Channels." The trail left by inter-office memos.

"Coordinator." The guy who has a desk between the two expediters.

"Consultant." Any ordinary guy more than 50 miles from home.

"To activate." To Xerox and add more names to the memo.

"To implement a program." Hire more people and expand the office.

"Under active consideration." We are looking for it in the files.

"Re-orientation." Getting used to working again.

"Reliable source." The guy you just met.

"Informed source." The guy who told the guy you just met.

"Unimpeachable source." The guy who originated the rumor.

"Clarification." To fill in the background with so many details that the foreground goes underground.

"We are making a survey." We need more time to think of an answer.

"Note and initial." Let's spread the responsibility for this.

"Let's get together on this." I'm assuming you are as confused as I am.

# *Gold Brickers*

Timing is everything in life, especially in the business world. If it's pay-raise time and your boss says, "Let's talk turkey!"--that's good. If he says, "Let's talk, turkey"--that's not so good.

With all the unemployment it's amazing how many turkeys still hang on to their jobs. The other day in the office-supply store was the first time I've seen a secretary buy a six-pack of correction fluid. She's the type that thinks carbon forms are the time-saving device that allow you to make up to eight mistakes at the same time.

Then there are the turkeys with absentee problems. The boss knows something's wrong when people call in sick--three weeks in advance. One thing has always bothered me about being self-employed. Whom do you call when you're sick?

One employee at a local firm was always late to work. He said he couldn't sleep nights, so the boss told him to take some pills. He did and slept like a log. When the alarm rang, he dressed and went to work. "I didn't have a bit of trouble getting up this morning," he told the boss. "That's great," was the reply, "but where were you yesterday?"

Businessmen rarely know how their employees are going to react. The owner of a large business concern bought a number of signs reading: "DO IT NOW!" and had them hung around the various offices, hoping to inspire his people with promptness and energy in their work. One day soon afterwards a friend asked him how the scheme affected the staff.

"Well, not just the way I thought," he answered. "The cashier skipped with $30,000, the head bookkeeper eloped with the secretary and three clerks asked for a raise."

But there are those who stick to a job through thick and thin. An old friend visited us the other day, and we asked him how everything was going. He moaned, "My house burned down and it wasn't insured; my wife got run over by an uninsured car and she's in the hospital; my son's in jail; and my daughter's on LSD."

We said, "That's really tough. What are you doing these

days?" He said, "Same old thing--selling good luck charms."

## *Golden Years*

Life is nothing but snap, crackle and pop. When you're young, it's cereal. When you're old, it's your joints. I've been working all of my life, but somehow it seems longer. We're only young once. After that we have to think up a new set of excuses for our ineptitudes and follies.

If I had my life to live over again, I'd be a laboratory mouse. Think about it. They get free cigarettes; they keep their weight down with saccharine; they have bacon for breakfast, fried hamburgers for lunch, charcoal-broiled steaks for dinner. If they do get cancer, they're the first to get Laetrile.

Some people today are so afraid to die that they never begin to live. They're afraid of everything. Now they want to declare mother's milk unsafe, which will cause trouble. Particularly when they try to put on those warning labels.

When one learns how to make the most of life, most of it is gone. But the glory lies in its wealth of experience.

Modern times have done all right by me and mine, and I'm grateful for every gram of Salk vaccine, penicillin, tetanus serum, antibiotic, and aspirin; every box of detergent and jet-propelled cereal; for all vitamin capsules, cancer research, telephone service, indoor plumbing, fair-employment legislation, voting franchises, Social Security, and exploration of outer space. I am a long way from regarding this as the best of all possible worlds, but neither can I bring myself to think of it as irredeemable squalor.

It's not a perfect world. We haven't even been able yet to give the next generation a faucet that won't drip, but we pioneered the stratosphere and we leave the conquest of space to our grandchildren.

At my age an "acid trip" is going down to the drug store for a roll of Tums. I'm not sure what kind of insurance to take out--major medical or minor miracle. To me, putting on evening clothes means pajamas.

But don't call me an "old person". Dr. William B.Terhune, associate clinical professor of psychiatry, Yale School of Medicine, said, "If one would understand older people, one should first forget age. Oldness is not so much passing a certain birthday, as it is the rearrangement of a complicated set of physical, mental, social, and economic circumstances."

Dr. Terhune is right. We're in the middle of "re-arranging our circumstances." We live a well-balanced life. Prune juice on Monday, Wednesday and Friday--Kaopectate on Tuesday, Thursday, and Saturday. I feel like all my vital juices have turned to prune. I get the feeling my stomach is 20 years older than I am.

Continuing, Dr. Terhune says, "One must not label a man who has lived a lot of years as an old person. For an individual who has early formed good habits of living, picked up the important techniques of adjustment and acquired a good attitude or philosophy, life continues to be an ever-increasing adventure in development; development can continue at 60, 70, and 80 as surely as it did in youth.

Watch out, world, here I come! I'm working on those "important techniques of adjustment." I feel like picking up the phone, dialing my old office and calling in well. Oh, there are a few adjustments yet to make. I'm learning that when you're retired, money is like sex. You have to make a little bit go a long way. The nicest part about retirement is when paying income tax becomes a spectator sport.

There's good news and bad news. The good news is I still have lust in my heart. The bad news is, I have rust everywhere else.

# Golf/Tennis

Sunday is the day when we bow our heads. Some of us are praying and some of us are putting. I have a neighbor who is a firm believer in physical fitness. He's a firm believer in pumping iron. Mostly his number five iron. He goes to a very patriotic golf course. Every time he calls them to reserve a starting time, their answer is, "Oh, say, can you tee by the dawn's early light?"

My neighbor's wife came home from playing golf with her husband and she was very depressed. She said, "I did everything wrong. Wrong, wrong, wrong! I hit into the woods. I got caught in a sand trap. I hooked every drive. I missed three easy putts. And worst of all--I won!"

When I was trying to learn to play golf I had a very diplomatic pro who kept saying that I had a nice, fluid swing--after I'd landed in the water. But I finally gave up golf. I hit a spectator in the head with a golf ball--which was particularly embarrassing because I was putting at the time.

I've decided to play tennis. They say there are now 35 million tennis players in the United States. Wrong! There are 165 tennis players. The rest are waiting for courts.

I have a little advice for the beginner in tennis. It is an incredibly strenuous game that calls for chasing a ball with a racquet for hours on end--so it's best to start off with mixed doubles. Get a tray full of drinks and watch.

The three most important things to develop in your tennis game are a strong serve, a good backhand, and a convincing limp to explain why you lost.

I went into a sporting goods shop the other day and told the proprietor I was taking up tennis and I'd need some equipment. So he sold me a pair of shoes for $70, three cans of balls for $25, a book of tennis tips for $15, a sweat band for $8, and a year's membership in a tennis club for $500. Just as I was leaving I realized I had forgotten the most important thing. I said, "Could you supply me with a racquet?" He said, "Of course"--and he sold me a half interest in the shop.

But I still kinda like golf. It's a marvelous sport. Where else could you spend the afternoon with three hookers--score--and your wife doesn't get mad?

## Graduation

A graduation ceremony is where the commencement speaker tells 2,000 students dressed in identical caps and gowns that individuality is the key to success. That's when a kid gets his first touch of reality--all those students in the senior class, but only one is voted "most likely to succeed."

The best degrees are ones in specific areas, like psychology, engineering, and business administration. At least you know what kind of work you're out of. July is when a lot of students receive another commencement address--the location of the unemployment office. The way the new batch of graduates is being received by business and industry, some of them must be getting the feeling their degrees come from Who U?

Every year American colleges and universities graduate a few million Liberal Arts majors. It is upgrading our way of life. You don't know what a thrill it is to see your kid filling out an unemployment form in Latin. One young man who had just received his college degree rushed out and said, "Here I am world. I have an A.B.!" And the world replied, "Sit down, son, and I'll teach you the rest of the alphabet."

College has become a great expense. Two fathers were discussing the daughters in their respective families.

"What do you think," said one. "Should I send my daughter to college or not?"

"Well, I'll tell you my experience. It may help you to decide. It cost me $10,000 a year to send Penelope to college and it took her four years to capture a husband. I spent twelve hundred dollars to send Alice to the beach for three weeks, and she came home married. I recommend the beach."

## *Grandparent's Day*

Did you ever hear of "Grandparent's Day?"

Now, that's a laugh. It'll never get off the ground in a society of broken families where thousands of kids have a hard time figuring out who their parents are, much less grandparents. Here's a holiday that will horrify today's young mother. She has adjusted to believing she's "over the hill" at 30, only to wake up one morning with the terrifying thought, "My God! I'm going to be a grandmother!"

Today's grandparents have a hard time keeping score in the game of kids. Since becoming grandparents we've thrown everything we learned in child psychology right out the window.

Kids are different today. We have a grandson at the awkward age. He likes girls, but he doesn't know why.

You can't believe the outfit our neighbor's granddaughter came home with. Her grandfather asked, "Where in the world did you get that?" She said, "An Army-Navy store." He said, "Whose side?" Her face always looks like she made it up on a roller coaster. The soles of her shoes are four inches high. She looks halfway between demure and deformed.

Grandchildren today are very concerned with "finding themselves." So were we. If we wanted to find ourselves at the dinner table, we went out and got a job. When we were kids, all food was health food. If we didn't eat it our mothers would belt us. Our parents were strict. We had to be in by 10 and out by 21.

It's not that we don't respect our grandchildren; they're very intelligent and everyone keeps telling them how smart they are. But, as kids, the most dangerous thing we ever did was when we played bubble gum roulette. Six kids blew bubble gum in your face and one of them had the mumps.

Probably what shocks grandparents today is the fact most of the desperate crimes of violence in this country are becoming chiefly the work of youngsters under 21. If this is so, one is impelled to wonder what has happened to a nation of adults--this or any other--which allows itself to be terrorized by its own young. Grandparents day? Maybe it's time for another Armistice Day.

## *Grandfather's Questions*

When you tell a waiter you need a little more time to read the menu, is there any reason why he has to leave the building?

Why do we say, "Gesundheit!" whenever someone sneezes? Why are we bothering God when He has so many important things to do?

Why is the "walk light" at intersections timed for only

three seconds? To lure senior citizens to the center where they'll be better targets?

Why do TV weathermen always show a satellite picture of the world 10,000 miles away? Can you tell whether or not to wear a sweater from that altitude?

Why do they call them "No Nonsense Panty Hose?" Is there some weird nonsense that usually goes on inside them?

Why do they put headlights on vacuum sweepers? So you can vacuum in the dark and scare hell out of the cat?

Why are they brewing alcohol-free beer? Who's that for- -people who don't like to get drunk, but like to urinate?

Why do they call them "Grape Nuts"? There's no nuts and no grapes.

Where do they get K-Y Jelly? From Kentucky?

Why do girls wear make-up when they go to the beach? If a guy doesn't notice your half-naked body, false eyelashes aren't going to help.

Why do they consider "Tractor Pull" a sport? Is it because the rules of wrestling have become too complicated?

Why do some folks become lost in thought? Is it because it's such unfamiliar territory?

What's the meaning of "Be Alert?" Does it mean the world needs more lerts?

Do we need all these electronic games? It now costs more to amuse a child than it once did to educate his father.

Why do they call it a "fanny?" Because it's goose flesh?

Why do women always complain about their weight when they're eating?

Why don't dogs step in dog doo? They have four legs-- we have only two and we can't miss.

Why is it that when God makes fools he makes them on such a grand scale?

When women know someone is waiting, why do they say, "Just a minute?" That could mean any time from now until the earth shifts on its axis.

Does the 5-50 Protection Plan mean that your car's warranty expires at 10 'til 6 o'clock?

When people greet you with, "What's happening?" how specific should your answer be?

Do women always go to the bathroom together to help each other out of those tight pants?

Why do they call it "rush hour traffic" when your car just sits there?

When the dentist tells you that you're grinding your teeth at night, is it okay to fill your mouth with coffee beans and set the alarm for 7:30 a.m.?

If a 53-year-old man marries a 19-year old girl, and his son is dating the bride's mother and plans to marry her, does that mean the young man will become his dad's father-in-law?

Why do cat lovers always tell you their cat is "different?" If my cat always lands on his feet is it because I don't know how to throw him?

How do we know they have improved the taste of dog food? If this is true, why does my garbage always please him better?

If it's okay for a bartender to cut off a drunk, why can't a waiter cut off someone who's eating too much?

Why is it that honor students are always the ones found dead? Did you ever see a headline, "Drop-out Found Dead?"

Why do weathermen refer to the Midwest as "the nation's mid-section?" Is it because it's about 60 miles north of the pelvic area?

Why do people say, "Let's go, so we can get back...?" Why leave? They're already here.

The Eiffel Tower looks like it was built with an Erector

set. When are they going to finish it?

Can a cross-eyed person with dyslexia read?

Why do doormen have a union? If they go on strike, what will they do? Stand in front of their building?

Does a "crash diet" mean the person is not eating during an automobile accident?

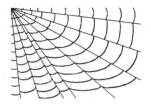

## *Halloween*

On October 31st strange people wearing masks will come to your door, and it's known as Halloween. In some parts of the country it's known as Monday--or Tuesday--or Wednesday--or....

New York is probably the worst place in the country for Halloween. Kids ring the doorbell and by the time you look through the peep-hole, open three locks, slide back the bolt, unhook the chain, disconnect the burglar alarm, and leash the German shepherd--it's Christmas.

Halloween is different every where you go. One time we spent Halloween in Texas and a little kid knocked on the door. I said, "Do you have change for a dollar?" He said, "Mister, in Texas a dollar *is* change!"

Have you ever taken a good look at what kids are given to eat at Halloween? There are licorice sticks, marshmallows, candy bars, apples, bubble gum, popcorn, saltwater taffy, sugared peanuts, lollipops, jawbreakers, peppermint sticks, potato chips, fudge, doughnuts and cookies. All you have to do is look at it and you'll know what made Wyatt Earp. I remember when we went around on Halloween collecting candy, cookies and apples--and it was trick or treat. Now it's dinner.

It's not easy outfitting a kid for Halloween. A mother bought her son a $50 outfit to scare his friends and neighbors. The kid said, "Should I take off the price tag?" She said, "Leave it on. We'll scare your father too!" The costume was a sheet, a mask, and a witch's hat. I didn't know Tiffany sold sheets. Trick or treat is what the stores play in October.

Today we don't really need ghosts and goblins to scare us. The Dow Jones average does a pretty good job--or the man in a black suit who comes for the IRS. Our friends are having a recession Halloween party. They have a big tub of water and we'll bob for I.O.U.s. We're getting great at bobbing for apples--our problem is keeping our heads above water.

Halloween is the only night of the year rock stars look natural--even Phyllis Diller looks right.

Halloween's the time when little girls love to get dressed up in their mother's old clothes. Unfortunately, little boys can't get dressed up in their father's old clothes--'cause he's still wearing them.

Isn't it amazing how expensive Halloween costumes have become? I saw a little witch's outfit for $29. I said, "Twenty-nine dollars? That's ridiculous!" The clerk said, "What's so ridiculous? It's made from an imported design, custom-tailored, hand-stitched, and a fine yarn." I said, "Yes, and you tell it well!"

I've noticed many of the Halloween costumes are inspired by the movie, "Star Wars." Last year one little kid came to the door dressed as a robot. I didn't know whether to give him an apple, a candy bar, or STP.

With all the horror movies today you wonder if there's anything scary left for Halloween. The thing that puzzles me about Frankenstein movies is the way the monster always walks around with his arms outstretched. I haven't seen anybody walk like that since my wife fell asleep under a sun lamp. Actually, the Frankenstein monster has a deep psychological problem. He thinks people are staring at him. They wanted to put him in analysis, but the way he moves it would have taken 45 minutes just to get to the couch.

We don't hear too much about Dracula any more 'cause he's suffering from an embarrassing condition. Especially for a vampire. It's called--loose dentures! Yes, thanks to upper-plate wobble, Dracula now has three big worries: A cross, a stake through his heart, and a tough throat.

Have you noticed how popular the word "killer" has become? There are killer bees, killer earthquakes, killer sharks. Now there's a new movie that will strike fear into the heart of every housewife--KILLER DUST!

If your doorbell doesn't ring on Halloween, you can depend that the kids have gone to the movies. Sometimes I keep having this terrible thought: What if the Muppets are real and we aren't?

## *Health Secrets*

Medical science has developed so amazingly within the past few years that it is now almost impossible for a doctor to find anything all right about a patient. The motto of the old-fashioned practitioner was, "I treat what you've got." Today it seems to be, "You've got what I treat."

I have gathered from many medical articles that the secret of health is still a secret. But Americans will try anything. Years ago it was said, "Early to bed and early to rise makes a man healthy, wealthy, and wise." We determined it also makes him socially dead. A doctor once said, "The best way to enjoy perfect health is to rise at five every morning and have a cold bath." We said, "Oh, well, what's the next best way?" Then there was, "An apple a day keeps the doctor away," but he just hung around until we made it into hard cider.

Today dieting is the thing. What's on the table eventually becomes what's on the chair. We have diet pills, diet drinks, diet dinners, diet doctors, and diet magazines. The whole world is fat! What a world! By the time you're important enough to take two hours for lunch, the doctor tells you to eat yogurt--that's a magical joining together of three vital ingredients: inspired advertising, imaginative flavoring and library paste.

Everybody has become food conscious. If some people were at the Last Supper, they'd be worrying about calories.

Mark Twain had much experience with physicians and said, "The only way to keep your health is to eat what you don't want, drink what you don't like, and do what you'd druther not." One doctor told Mark Twain, "I can't quite diagnose your case--I think it's drink." Twain replied, "All right, doctor. I'll come back some time when you're sober."

We can't quite figure out this diet craze, whether it's for the sake of health or appearance. Americans soon will be looking like a million dollars--all in loose change. Dieting isn't really all that tough. It is not difficult for a person to watch what he eats. The tough part of dieting is watching what other people are eating.

# Home Sweet Home

You have to admire the American spirit. Where else but in America can somebody borrow a $10,000 down payment from a relative, get a $60,000 first mortgage, a $30,000 second mortgage and be called a homeowner?

We went out with a real estate broker to look at houses. It's interesting how many people now have names for their houses. We looked at one place for $135,000 and the name over the door was Rolling Meadow. We looked at another place for $185,000 and the name over the door was Stately Manor. And you might find this hard to believe, but we looked at a house for $18,000 and even that had a name over the door--Fido.

It's amazing how small the new houses are. We looked at one that advertised a cathedral ceiling in the living room. I said, "Cathedral ceiling? It's eight feet high." The broker said, "Right. You take one look at it and say, "Good God!"

Remember when the biggest problem was paying off the mortgage instead of getting one? We've now reached the Seven Dwarfs stage of taking out a mortgage. When you go to a lending institution, you're Bashful. When you hear that mortgages are still available, you're Happy. When you're told the interest rate, you're Grumpy. If you accept it, you're Dopey.

I finally figured out what the broker meant when he said our house just needed TLC--Tender Loving Cash. I know a professional comedian who went back to selling houses because it's so much easier. To get a laugh all you have to do is give the price. In 1932, some friends of ours bought an eight room house in downtown Houston for $2,500. And they just had it listed--on the New York Exchange.

We learned why the new houses feature an eat-in kitchen. By the time you finish paying for one you don't have enough money to eat out.

Nowadays, it's easy to spot a new house. It's the one with the small rooms and the large payments. I asked a ballpark estimate on a house and got a fair price-- to buy a ballpark. We may be going back to the concept of three generations living in the same house. It'll take that many to pay for it.

I went to a real estate broker and I said, "Look, I don't need a big expensive house. All I really need is a roof over my head, a place to sleep, and a bathroom. Do you have anything like that for about $25,000?"

He said, "Sure--a tent, a cot, and a shovel."

With the mixed-up sociological structure of our times, I'm beginning to wonder if the importance of owning your own home will ever be as strong as in years past. For example: The size of the American family is rapidly diminishing. It's reached the point, says the Census Bureau, where we average less than one child per household. In 1970, the average American household consisted of 3.14 persons. Last year, it was down to 2.75 persons.

A real estate agent was trying to get a modern young woman, newly married, interested in the purchase of a home. She laughed as she said, "A home? What do I need with a home? I was born in a hospital, educated in a college, courted in an automobile, and married in a church. I live out of cans and paper bags, I spend my mornings on the golf course, my afternoons at work, and my evenings at the movies. And when I die, I'll be buried from the undertaker's parlor. All I need is a garage."

There may be more truth than poetry in that little yarn.

Twenty-three percent of all households in 1980 consisted of one person living alone. There were 17.8 million one-person households last year!

The government also has an effective solution for housing problems, just for veterans. It's called re-enlistment.

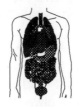

## *Hospitals*

Whatever happened to good old-fashioned medicine? I can remember when the first thing that happened when you were rushed to a hospital was, they took your pulse. Now what they take is your Blue Cross number. As anyone who has ever been in a hospital knows, the road to recovery is a toll road.

The bills you get from a hospital are always interesting. Most of the time they're in the form of a computer print-out. A computer, I'll add, that got programmed at a used car lot.

Everything on a hospital bill is itemized. You look up at your I.V. and you know the bottle is costing you $19.75. I always figure for $19.75 the least they could do is dress it up. Add a touch of garlic, a sprig of parsley, and an olive.

Everything is so expensive. What hospitals really need is cheaper equipment--like an X-ray machine that takes four poses for a quarter.

But I happen to know that hospitals are trying to conserve. If you don't believe it, look at the hospital gowns they give you to wear. For those of you who have never seen a hospital gown, it's sort of an intensive bare unit. I don't know who came up with the design for the first hospital gown, but I think it was the Fernwood Flasher. I don't know of anyone who feels comfortable in a hospital gown. How could you? The front is rated G and the back is rated X. Now I know what southern exposure means.

The real agony of hospitals is, everybody is running around half-naked and you're too sick to look--that's how they tell if you're getting well. The first time you do a double-take--out!

In the area of conservation, one of the things hospitals are doing is recycling the food. I had a hamburger that was so old, you didn't season it--you dusted it.

If you're a fella, there's always a lot of fantasy attached to things that happen in hospitals, like back-rubs. A hospital back-rub is like a massage parlor run by feminists.

I believe in the time-honored home remedies. If you caught pneumonia, you took aspirin, hot tea, chicken soup, and you died. Now what could be more simple than that?

## *Income Tax*

Income tax time rolls around every spring. This year the government claims the forms are so simple even a three-year old can understand them. Providing he's a C.P.A. If you read the income tax instructions carefully, you realize there are only two ways to fill out the form--and they are both wrong. I bought one of those books on "How to Fill Out Your Income Tax" and they're great. It gives you something to read while the accountant is doing your tax.

Nothing ever changes much. In the thirties, it was the Depression that kept us out of good restaurants. In the nineties, it's the Internal Revenue Service. Do you realize that the IRS is the only outfit that really knows what to give the person who has everything? An audit!

Sometimes I get the feeling that when an employee of the Internal Revenue Service comes to work with an upset stomach, a headache, and an general out of sorts feeling, they immediately transfer him over to the auditors' section. And they're so subtle when they call you down for a tax audit. The Muzak is playing, "Your Cheatin' Heart."

They called one fellow down for listing himself as a single man with child. They said, "This must be a misconception." He said, "You're telling me!" Another man was called for audit because he listed three blondes under Living Expenses. They asked him, "That's Living?" And he said, "You'd better believe it!"

I feel every man should have at least one shabby, threadbare, worn-out suit for income-tax audits.

You could make a fortune these days if you could come up with a product that's low-priced, habit forming, and deductible--and everybody is searching for deductions. One taxpayer deducted $2,000 because he had water in his basement. Then they found out he lived in a houseboat. An architect bought his wife a bra and deducted it as a Structural Improvement. Another totaled his church contributions by saying, "I gave $2 last Sunday, $2 on Christmas. and $2 on Thanksgiving. That's $222.

## Inflation

It's just amazing how many Americans have green thumbs. It's from counting out twenties at the supermarket. There's even a new sign at our supermarket's checkout counter. It says: ENGLISH & SPANISH SPOKEN HERE. TEARS UNDERSTOOD.

We may have reached a critical stage in food prices. The other day I saw someone put a lettuce leaf in the Xerox machine. Lettuce is the green on the plate you substitute for the green in your wallet.

I've come to the conclusion that kids are naturally perverse. Remember when you could never get a kid to eat a salad? So now that the price of lettuce, celery, and tomatoes has gone through the roof, what do they become? Vegetarians!

Food is getting so costly toothpicks come with instructions. Meat is so high, I just bought two pounds of bacon--on the layaway plan. For a buck and a half you don't get pork chops any more--pork chips.

## *January*

The holiday season always seems to end up the same way. In December it's, "Ho! Ho! Ho!" And in January it's "Owe! Owe! Owe!"

I always get a little sentimental about January. It's the month when you're in your lowest possible tax bracket.

In January, you buy $45 worth of Christmas cards at half price-which you won't be able to locate next December.

January is when you order the flower seeds you plant in April and wonder what happened to them in August.

In January, that cooler weather you prayed for back in July finally makes it.

And January is when the President goes on TV to tell us the State of the Nation--and you realize it's a re-run.

I love these cold winter mornings when there's a real nip in the smog. Having spent a good part of the last six months pushing a lawn mower, I look forward to winter. Winter is nature's way of freezing your grass off.

It's great to live in the sun country and read about the tough winters in the other states. Frostbite is a real problem in Buffalo. Last week, a rock 'n roll singer showed up at a hospital with a finger missing. The doctor asked, "How in the world did you lose a finger?"

"I dunno, man. I'm standing at this bus stop--the

temperature's fifteen below zero. I figure I'll rehearse one of my numbers while I'm waiting. So I snap my fingers like this--Ooops, there goes another one!"

If anyone comes up to me again and tells me the winters aren't as cold as they used to be, I'm going to hit him with the biggest thing I can find--my gas bill!

## *Jogging Jaws*

Our future as a nation is going to depend not so much on what happens in outer space, as what happens in inner space--the space between our ears.

We should be thankful we live in a country where we can say what we think without thinking. However, getting some people to stop talking is like finding the end of a roller towel. They seem to listen with their mouths. What the world needs is more open minds and fewer open mouths.

The most arresting advice we ever encountered was this, "If you want to be popular, live so that a blind person would like you. Lasting popularity depends not on a pretty face or being handsome, but inner qualities that commun-icate themselves to others through media other than sight."

We asked a blind friend to explain that bit of advice. She said these personality assets "are expressed through such things as a gentle voice, persistent friendliness, small kindnesses, thoughtfulness of another's tender ego, deserved praise, and excursions in encouragement."

She was saying that God gave man five senses--touch,

taste, smell, sight, and hearing. The successful person is endowed with two more--horse and common.

There's a lot of Jogging Jaws going around today-- people running off at the mouth. Jawboning may be all right, but sometimes the bone is in another part of the head. The only exercise these people get is jumping to conclusions.

We're always a little suspicious of people who say, "As God is my witness." We're never sure if it's for the defense or the prosecution. You'll usually find these people "me- deep" in conversation. Some people bring happiness wherever they go; the egoist, whenever they go. The closest they'll ever get to a brainstorm is a light drizzle--yet, because they're loud and have jumper cables on their tongues they spread a lot of worrisome baloney.

Maybe we'd better stop complaining so much about what's wrong with this world--God might want to take it back to the shop!

## *July 4th Traffic*

The Fourth of July weekend is time for the National Safety Council to count the toll of dead, injured, and missing in action. It is true that our basic law says every American is entitled to "the pursuit of happiness"--but not at the rate of 80 miles an hour. Pioneer days may have had their dangers, but none of them compare with the modern practice of going around with one foot in the grave and the other on the accelerator.

The main problem lies in the fact many motorists drive as if the road belongs to them when they don't even own the car; they take the steering wheel and the speed laws into their own hands at the same time. It might help to make steering wheels in the shape of a harp.

Fast driving is just reckless driving that hasn't done it yet. Keeping up with the Joneses is not so harmful; it's when we try to pass them on a curve that things happen. Some motorists are in such a hurry to get into the next county that they go right into the next world.

One way to reduce motor accidents is to build cars so they can't go any faster than the average driver thinks; maybe it's time to stop improving the automobile and begin working on the brains of the driver. If you have trouble telling the front from the back of some of these new little cars, just notice the driver. Front is the way he isn't looking.

Travel makes strange hospital bedfellows. Be sure to insist on taking the right-of-way while driving. It will be a comfort to you in the hospital. People know exactly what to do 'til the doctor comes these days. They insist they were only going 20 miles an hour and had the right of way. What some people don't know about driving would fill a hospital. After witnessing an auto wreck they drive carefully for several blocks.

July Fourth we celebrate Americanism. Americanism today seems to mean that we spend two hours buying a life insurance policy and two-tenths of a second going through the grade crossing. A junk shop near a railroad crossing in Denver carries a sign with this hint to motorists, "Go ahead; take a chance. We'll buy the car."

## Kids' Questions

Kids ask all kinds of questions. Parents are supposed to come up with logical answers--but grandparents are not! It's a grandfather's prerogative to come up with some fantasy that's different from the answers of mother and dad; otherwise how will he be remembered?

Everything we read today is so factual and carefully documented that it's time to explode some undocumented fantasy. Grandfather is just the guy to light the fuse. Here's some fantasy designed to stimulate the aging mind and scare hell out of the grandchildren.

Question: Why do men go bald?

Answer: Because they wear hats. But science has discovered how to transplant hair cells onto rubber trees-- some day your car can have blonde, brunette, or red-headed tires that don't go bald.

Question: Why do trees live longer than people?

Answer: Because they have sap ducts instead of blood vessels. Science is working on inserting sap ducts in the human body so you can feed yourself through osmotic pressure in the bath tub using roast beef and gravy soap.

Question: What's the difference between plants and animals?

Answer: Plants make their own food out of sunlight and soil. Animals can't, yet. But we're working on that. Science has developed a dog with leafy ears and root claws. He can stand in the rain and get a full meal.

Question: Why are some birds colored?

Answer: They get tangled up in the waves of colored television. How do you think a pigeon reacts, leisurely flying along, when he bumps into an air wave filled with cowboys and Indians in bloody battle?

Question: What is a fly speck?

Answer: India ink. Science is crossing trained fleas, lightning bugs, mosquitos and flies to make a clever insect with its own light that tatoos interesting art upon command.

These are just a few suggestions for getting away from the Little Red Riding Hood and Ugly Duckling stuff. Heaven help us if the little darlings believe you!

## Kissing For Health

Bombarded by warnings about dawn-to-dusk dangers,

Americans are confused and concerned about the safety of the products they buy and the hazards of modern living.

Personally, I felt a lot more safe and secure back in 1933, when all I had to fear was fear itself. If medical science has made progress, why do I feel worse than I did twenty years ago? I knew I was over the hill when I quit looking at *Playboy* because holding open that center page aggravated my arthritis. I'm beginning to feel like my warranty is running out.

I just had my annual physical and the doctor says I'm as sound as a dollar, but he thinks I'll recover. I've always felt weak. It goes back to my childhood. You've heard of support stockings? I had a support diaper.

I'm quitting tranquilizers. I just read a news dispatch from Rome. "Kissing is good for your health and will make you live longer. Kissing stimulates the heart, which gives more oxygen to the body's cells, keeping the cells young and vibrant." The researchers also found that kissing produces antibodies in the human body, that in the long run, can protect the body against certain infections.

Now, *that's* a treatment I can stand. That sure beats acupuncture. Personally, I couldn't take acupuncture. I'm too squeamish. I need gas just to have my eyeglasses adjusted.

I may have some luck with the kissing treatment. Girls look on me as the strong, silent type. That's because I can't talk and hold in my stomach at the same time. But finding the right girl is a problem. The one with whom I wanted to share this medical experiment takes so many tranquilizers that if she breathes at you, you go limp.

They've also scientifically proved that laughing gives you a great internal workout. "New evidence shows humor may directly help fight pain and inflammatory conditions such as arthritis," they say. I don't think you'd better combine that with kissing, however. If you get that kiss, and then start laughing your fool head off, it could be fatal.

## *Kondon's*

For the past 30 years we've been using a very effective nasal jelly that has been on the market since 1889. It relieves sufferers from head colds, hay fever, and sinus allergies. You'll find it advertised in *The Old Farmer's Almanac*. Until this year we've never hesitated to recommend it in our conversations with fellow sufferers. Now we've found ourselves caught in a listener-versus-talker conflict with serious implications.

The product is produced by the Kondon Manufacturing Corporation, located in Croswell, Michigan. For some reason, through all these years, it has been named KONDON'S nasal jelly. No problem as long as you write the word as a prescription. Today, however, don't dare say the word unless you want all kinds of misunderstanding. Let me tell you what I mean:

Recently I was seated on a stool at our breakfast bar watching the painters re-texture our kitchen ceiling. Something in the air caused my allergies to kick-in and I started a rapid fire sneezing attack.

Wanting to be helpful, my dear wife Madeline said, "Sit still--I'll get the KONDON'S!"

One of the painters dropped his brush; the other damned near fell off the ladder. My God, we did it again. Ever since the uproar at Rotary Ladies Night, we had forgotten our plan to emulate those days when we were raising a family and said things like, "Don't give the b-a-b-y that damned c-a-n-d-y."

The deal at the Rotary dinner was the worst. In the midst of the meal at the Rio Rancho Inn, something set off my sneeze-alarm. I was covering my sneezes in a handkerchief and backing away from the table. Mama was scrambling through her purse, and as I rose from my chair to leave the room, she said, "Jack--you'd better take the KONDON'S with you!"

The guy across the table choked on a piece of meat, gasped for breath and was turning a funny shade of blue before someone popped him between the shoulder blades with a knock-out punch. With my sneezing and his gagging we came close to breaking up a festive occasion. That was the night we agreed to *never* speak that word.

I should have known a year ago that I was headed for trouble. I almost lost a good friend during a conversation concerning springtime allergies. He, too, is subject to rapid-fire sneezing. All I said was, "I just put some Kondon's up my nose." He started backing away from me, looked me squarely in the eyes and said, "My God, Jack, you can't tell me those things will stop hay fever, too!" I'm going to start studying linguistic communications.

## *Labor Day*

On Labor Day weekend American's hear the cry of the

open road. It's saying, "Stay home! Stay home!" With high-powered cars and dim-witted motorists, it is more danger-ous now to take your loved ones on the highway than it once was to fight to defend them from foreign aggression.

People by the thousands will take to the highways. The concrete cloverleaf has become our nation's flower. Labor Day is the last long weekend before school and the last chance of summer to move out with bag and baggage. Husbands will try to explain what a holiday is to their wives and explain what labor is to the kids.

Labor Day has lost its true intent and purpose. Gone are the days when bloody overalls mailed to a postoffice served as the working man's reminder of safety. Gone are the sweat shops. Today, athletes strike for six-digit salaries and government workers defy their loyalty oath by striking.

Today we bad-mouth free enterprise and our govern-ment to get more money.

Yes, the U.S. is in bad shape--in some respects worse off than any other country in the world. No other country is suffering political and economic troubles because of a surplus of wheat. No other country has traffic congestion because so many people own automobiles.

In no other country do workers make so much money, while good help is hard to find and harder to keep. In no other country do people take so many holidays, and work so few hours, so they will have time to spend their money. In no other country is obesity, caused by plenty of everything, and high living a chief medical problem. Yes, it's a sad situation.

To some people an occupational hazard today means being offered a job when they report to pick up their unemployment check. Things have become too easy for us. Our forefathers ran a farm with less machinery than we need to maintain a lawn.

## *Las Vegas*

I just came back from a glorious week in Las Vegas where I underwent a rather unusual operation. Had my wallet removed and they didn't even give me an anesthetic. I won't say I'm unlucky, but I lost $42 in a gum machine.

Maybe it was the temperature. The sun was too hot and the dice were too cold. But I did well in Las Vegas. Arrived in an $8,000 car and came back in a $40,000 bus.

Old proverbs are ridiculous. Take the one that goes, "There's safety in numbers."--You ever try Las Vegas? You can't really call Las Vegas a city. It's more like a garbage disposal for money.

They're very labor conscious in Vegas. You go there and right away you join the A.F.of L.--the American Federation of Losers.

You meet interesting people there. I met the one who invented round dice for people who'd rather shoot marbles. I met some atomic scientists who were there for rest and relaxation. One of them became caught up in the gambling whirl and spent all his time at the crap tables. After a while, two of his friends got a little worried. One said, "Look at poor Smythe--in there gambling like there's no tomorrow!" And the other one answered, "Maybe he *knows* something!" Those guys spent three days at the tables. Only went upstairs for a change of wallets.

Inflation has really changed things in Las Vegas. One fella won $75,000 and had to see if it would change his welfare payments. There are all kinds of ways to get rid of your money. They even sell the Irish Sweepstakes-- sometimes known as Las Vegas with a brogue. After they announce the winners, Internal Revenue is singing, "Did your money come from Ireland?"

The bookies are all heart too. At Little Big Horn they would have given you Custer and three points. One of them took a 9 to 5 job in Vegas. It wasn't a good job, but he liked the odds.

I learned one thing--the Red Cross isn't the only group that's out for blood!

## *Laughter - The Best Medicine*

In addition to the fact that laughter is the best medicine, it has three notable advantages: 1. It's by far more pleasant to take than most medicine. 2. You don't have to worry about getting an overdose. 3. It doesn't cost anything. 4. You don't have to see a specialist to get a prescription.

You can beat the blues--actually whip depression--with humor and laughter. It reduces tension and stress; humor can make you feel good inside. A smile, a voice, a sense of humor and personality are the best weapons of a human today. Life without humor is like an automobile without springs. Boredom is a symptom of hardening of the brain. Humor is the jockey that rides our nightmares away.

Here are some simple tips on how to banish depression: Know what makes you laugh--and surround yourself with those things. Seek out those things that are humor sources for you, even if it's a Laurel and Hardy film.

Take a humor break--and share it with family, friends, or co-workers. This will make you feel better about yourself. If you get someone else to laugh, that only increases your good feelings.

Laugh at life's everyday mishaps. You can't control them, so it's better for you to laugh than to sit there and make yourself sick. So, if someone accidentally splatters your sparkling kitchen floor with a couple of raw eggs, just smile and say, "Well, that's certainly one way of making scrambled eggs."

When you're with friends, share laughs instead of worries. Take the time to inject humor into your life. The mood of joy is the mood of health.

Whence comes this idea having fun can't be God's will? The God who made giraffes, a baby's fingernails, a puppy's tail, a crook-necked squash, the bobwhite's call, and even a young girl's giggle, has a sense of humor.

## *Lib Language*

In recent news reports leaders of the feminine liberation movement express a degree of disappointment in achieving their goals during the past 20 years. We're not familiar with all of their goals, but we must admit they certainly succeeded in messing up the English language!

Abolition of sexist language was one of their first goals. Nursery rhymes, school books, magazines, newspapers--all things written or spoken were targets. The argument was made that sexist language was "causing great pain and suffering to women" and that true equality could never be attained until all masculine words were eliminated.

The proponents tossed out "man" and substituted "person"--a witlessness that brought a lot of confusion. One woman spent a whole year working on a National Organization for Women assignment to hunt through thousands and thousands of greeting cards to flush out "sex bias."

The first world-shaking word to go was mankind. According to Roget's *International Thesaurus,* "mankind" has become "personkind." Human beings, the human race, humans collectively--which is what mankind is--will lose the denominative identity it has had since the world began.

Chairman has become chairperson. Confusion still reigns in more than one presiding officer's chair. I've heard, "chairlady, chairperson, madam chairman," and "the chair."

I was sitting in a maternity hospital when a nurse came in, walked up to a fellow next to me and said, "Congratulations! It's a person!"

It's always fascinating going to a feminist meeting. Where else can you hear the first ten amendments of the constitution referred to as the "Jill" of Rights?

There is no such thing as a little bit of purge. To make the anti-sexism concept a workable reality the entire male connection, in every detail, would have to be eliminated. Did anyone notice that the last three letters of "person" spell a masculine word? We would have to drop off every "person" midway and be left with "per". Personkind would have to be perkind, and the mailperson a mailper.

# Love

"It is regrettable," a psychologist says, "that there is no adequate test for love at first sight." Yeah? Present-day love at first sight is based on more information than a year's acquaintance in the past. Love at first sight is possible, but it is always well to wipe off your spectacles and take a second good look.

A critic says that modern fiction runs too much to love. Yes, and modern love runs too much to fiction. Love doesn't really make the world go round. It just makes people dizzy so it looks like it. All's fair in love and war. They are also alike in other ways.

No other co-educational institution equals matrimony. It is usually a happy marriage if he will give and she will forgive. A successful marriage is one where the wife is the boss, but doesn't know it. The modern woman's idea of being a real helpmate is to thread the needle for her husband when he sews on his button.

Looking after a husband is like playing a game of cards. You must play what is dealt you. The glory consists not so much in the winning as in playing a poor hand well. A husband is like an egg--if kept continually in hot water he becomes hard boiled.

Many a wife hides her husband's faults; but that's no reason for always keeping her busy at the job. A girl never believes a man who says he is not worthy of her until after she is married. Couples used to marry for better or worse; now it's for more or less.

A model marriage is one in which the wife is a treasure

and the husband is a treasury. A woman will usually forgive a husband's past if he comes home with a present.

It's never a happy marriage unless both get better mates than they deserve. When a wife wishes she had gone for a career instead of marriage, you can bet she doesn't wish it half so much as her husband does.

We don't say that marriages are not made in heaven, but if they are, heaven needs a new shipping clerk, one who won't get the wrong address on so many.

# *Marriage*

People ask me how we've stayed married for so long--50 years. Here's the secret: My wife and I go to a lovely romantic restaurant twice a week. A little candlelight, a little wine. She goes Tuesdays, I go Thursdays!

Marriages today don't last long. You know the marriage didn't work when the thank-you notes for the presents are signed by an attorney. A marriage contract with a retirement plan would be interesting.

You think you have troubles? My neighbor has three kids and not one of them looks like him. The oldest one looks like the plumber. The middle one looks like the postman. And the youngest one is only five years old and already wants to sell insurance.

Families are all mixed up. One day two kids in our neighborhood were fighting. The first little boy said, "My daddy can beat your daddy!" The second said, "Forget it. My daddy IS your daddy." It is horrifying to think what the next generation will have to do to shock its parents.

The world's hardest job is parenthood. Its simplicities have long since departed, only its intricacies remain. It is a staggering task to maintain family unity in a world of transition, division, and license. No insurance company has ever issued a policy against the possibility of being a bad parent--the risks are too great. That's why many of today's young parents simply go bananas.

Dr. Marynia F. Farnham, psychiatrist and author says, "There is one type of woman rarely seen in a psychiatrist's office. That is the woman who is glad she is a woman. Although now in a minority in our female population (only 34.4% according to a survey made by *Fortune* Magazine), she honestly enjoys homemaking and more than anything in the world wants to raise a family of healthy, normal youngsters. During my 20 years of listening to distressed patients, I have never met her in my office."

Young couples should do a lot of looking before they leap. You know you're in trouble if your license is stamped: Corrective Eyeglasses Required--and it's your marriage license.

## *Men*

A movie actress says she's looking for a perfect man to marry. She can locate quite a number by reading tombstones, but she can't marry them. There's no such thing as a "perfect man."

Man is that consistent animal who can get a hearty laugh out of pictures in an old family album and then look in the mirror without so much as a grin. He laughs with amused condescension at the very idea of eyelash curlers, then spends ten minutes trying to coax a couple of wisps of hair across a bald spot.

Maybe it's the "clean-cut American look" myth to

pretend that shaving isn't an ordeal, but shaving is an ornery chore for men. Other languages admit it, but our TV commercials glamorize it. Our "shave" is defined "to remove hair close to the skin with a sharp instrument." The German "shaben" means to scrape or plane; Danish "skave" and Icelandic "skafa" mean to scratch. The Greek for shave means "to dig." Lithuania's "skapoti" translates as "cut or hollow out," and the Russian "kopati" implies scarifying with a bulldozer. You can't judge a man by his facial foliage.

Neither can you judge a man by the clothes he wears. God made one, the tailor the other, and you can make the average man mad by referring to him as the average man.

The question is not whether man descended from monkey, but when is he going to quit descending? Science might relax about the origin of man and work on determining his finish. He's sort of a roadhouse where his ancestors stop on their way to being his descendants.

Some men think they have an inferiority complex when, in fact, they are inferior. Self-made men quit the job too soon. But they usually admire their maker.

Men are of two classes: those who do their best work today and forget about it; and those who promise to do their best work tomorrow--and forget about it. Will Rogers said, "God made man a little lower than angels, and he has been getting a little lower ever since."

## *Missiles*
Everybody has missiles on their mind. We have all

kinds of demonstrations and protest songs. Have you taken a good look at these kids who said, "Make love, not war?" Most of them looked like they'd flunk at either.

I wonder if the President ever feels inadequate, listening to these kids sing their protest songs? Let's face it. Not only do they have the answer to every problem facing the world today--but it rhymes, too. You think it's easy writing these protest songs? What rhymes with Armageddon?

I can understand how they feel. On the other hand, I'm kinda glad we didn't face the British at Lexington with "Jimmy Crack Corn and I Don't Care!"

The British and American governments will never ban the bomb. They couldn't take the risk of five million students with nothing to do after classes. But I can't understand why students in foreign countries are so quick to attack the U.S. embassy every time the weatherman predicts rain. Washington is now working on a prefabricated U.S. embassy building for the smaller Asian countries. It comes with the windows already broken. Foreigners can't help but be impressed by our affluence. There are building shortages all over the world--while we have buildings to vandalize and burn.

I must admit, however, the Government is doing some wild missile tests. They send up one of our rockets--then they send up one of our missiles to shoot it down. And what does this prove? It proves if Cape Canaveral ever declares war on us, we're safe. The last time I visited the Cape I saw them fire a Polaris missile. It's incredible. Imagine being released from a submarine, coming up through 3,000 feet of water, shooting 30,000 feet into the air, then without a second's hesitation heading straight for Moscow! And every night, I see people getting lost on a detour in Albuquerque.

People are getting very uptight about all the political

fiddling with MX missiles, nuclear warheads, nuclear "freeze," and war scares. Fortunately, my wife puts all of these things in perspective. She said, "Can you imagine if all 60,000 nuclear warheads went off at the same time? If would be just my luck to be baking a sponge cake!"

## Modern Music

The other night we went to dinner where there was a musical group that took the rest out of restaurant and put the din in dinner. If you don't think there's a generation gap just remember when three little words meant, "I Love You." Today it's, "Yeah! Yeah! Yeah!" Nowadays, if you get the D.T.s--you don't know whether to get a doctor and get cured, or a guitar and get rich.

You know what's wrong with the world today? Guns have silencers when it's electric guitars that need them. One of the singers we heard had a terrible experience. Right in the middle of her big number, she remembered the melody.

Next week they're going to have a very unusual singing group--the Four Switchblades. They've already cut five records and a cop. They have a very unusual singing style. One of them loses the melody and the other three help him look for it.

I love a beat. I even snap my fingers to windshield wipers. But listening to last week's group was the first time I ever heard finger snapping carry the melody. It's the movements they go through that intrigue me--sort of a coordinated fit. And they carry a truckload of electronic gear-tweeters from Hartz Mountain and woofers from the American Kennel Club.

Folk songs are fun. Frankly, I'm a little suspicious of these authentic folk songs they're digging up. At latest count, there are at least 18,742,000 folk songs around. A hundred years ago, there weren't even that many folks. They say folk music is the living expression of a people. What people do you know who spend their lives stomping on the floor and singing through their nose? I'm not knocking folk singers, mind you. Anyone who can turn an adenoid condition into a million dollars earns my respect.

Do you realize, if airline ticket sellers didn't put our phone calls on "hold", most people today wouldn't know what good music is?

# *Money*

A lot of folks today spend money they haven't earned to buy things they don't need to impress people they don't like. Most of us don't want the government to squander our money because we want to do it ourselves.

In the good old days the man who saved money was a miser. Now he's a wonder. Saving is a simple matter. You just buckle down and make money faster than your family can spend it. A system of checks and balances is all right if you have the balances for the checks.

"There's no money in heaven," declares an evangelist. This probably explains why so many people go to hell trying to get some. They say that money talks; about all it says to most of us is "good-bye."

The only thing which keeps the average man's wallet from being flat these days is that it is packed full of credit cards. The Roman goddess of prosperity and plenty was called Abundantia. We have a new name for this goddess today. We call her credit card. The credit card is the magic key that opens the door to prosperity and plenty. No wonder so many people get their exercise by running wildly into debt. The man or woman who is the proud possessor of a credit card can say with deep feeling, "All that I am, or all that I ever hope to be, I owe...."

This brings to mind a sign in the window of a gift shop

which offered this suggestion, "For the man who has everything--a calendar to remind him when the payments are due."

It's easier to run up a bill than to run down the money to pay for it. Once when a family was well off and lived in luxury their friends said that they "lived off the fat of the land." Today most families--whether well off or not--live in luxury and manage to do it by living off the cuff.

Money doesn't mean everything, but everything seems to mean money. Wouldn't it be nice to have all the money you've spent foolishly so you could spend it foolishly again? It has been said, "Money is the root of all evil". That must be why we all try to dig it up. Experts claim it goes farther than it did. It also stays away longer.

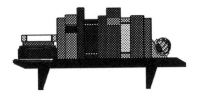

## *Morals*

The modern reader, explains a commentator of literary trends, distrusts concealed morals in fiction. He needn't worry. Most of the characters in the recent fiction don't seem to have any morals to conceal. Modern writers ought to lift their minds out of the gutter. After all, we must keep our gutters clean. A lot of today's writing is just an ash tray filled with butts and stubs of thought.

Talk about a double standard of morality usually refers to a double standard of immorality. The most significant thing about our code of morals today is its elasticity.

Everybody today is supposed to have an open mind. Some so-called open minds should be closed for repairs.

Many think they have open minds when they're merely vacant. They're able to detect a rattle in their cars more quickly than one in their heads.

The objection to an open mind these days is that convictions get out as often as new ideas get in. Some who have these so-called open minds let the wrong kind of stuff get in; maybe they're too porous to hold a conviction.

Our present social morals constantly bargain with our future life and the hereafter. Someday we must come face to face with the fact that our lives have been lived. What we have done is behind us and cannot be changed. We are like the sightseer who turned to the elevator operator and asked, "What would happen if something went wrong with the elevator? Would we keep going up or go down?"

The elevator operator looked over the tourist slowly and drawled, "That would depend on the way you have lived."

# *News Commentary*

SAN FRANCISCO--A newlywed couple reported having sex when the earthquake struck. "Fortunately, we were standing in the doorway," the bride said.

BOSTON--A new diet book suggests eating nothing but fruit until 12:00 noon. Then don't plan anything until 8:00 p.m.--in fact you can finish reading the diet book while sitting on the toilet.

MIAMI--School Principal Alan Small reports a grade school student has just finished reading a 400-page book-- That's a lot of coloring. No doubt he had crayon cramp for awhile.

ANCHORAGE--A beach comber says he knew the oil tanker was in trouble when he found a bottle stuffed with an S.O.S. pad.

DALLAS--GloriaMiller is filing suit against her doctor for undressing her, feeling her breasts and hugging her. She was still in the waiting room.

SAN ANTONIO--Jeff Mutton is asking for a divorce because his wife believes in reincarnation. She says she was rich in her former life and is still spending money like she had it.

ALBUQUERQUE--JuanHernandez Garcia was arrested for child abuse. He came home drunk, beat up the wife and kids, then discovered he was in the wrong apartment. Juan Hernandez Garcia is single.

NEW YORK--Some of the finer hotels are now placing fluorescent condoms on bed tables--just in case someone forgets to turn on the lights.

DENVER--The driver of a car was thrown through the windshield after crashing into a bridge railing. He was charged with leaving the scene of an accident.

BOSTON--Researchersnow say having sex can overtax your heart. (I used to think that the coolest way to die would be having sex. Then I decided I didn't want a woman walking around with that much self confidence.)

DETROIT--A new smoke alarm has been invented. It has a snooze button that lets you sleep in.

NEW YORK--*Cosmopolitan* magazine says that a sense of humor is the first thing women look for in a man. I don't believe that. Who do you want in your bra--Tom Selleck or the three stooges?

CHICAGO--Science Fair winners were announced today. However, a few questions remain concerning marketability. Winners included a toilet tank drop that turns the water yellow, pancake flavored syrup, radio dinners, and bell-bottom panty hose for girls with big feet.

## *New Year's Eve*

Everyone enjoys getting ready for New Year's Eve. I know because I just got in a supply of bourbon-flavored Tums. New Year's Eve is sort of a target date--for throwing out the tree and 50 percent of the toys that were under it.

I have one big problem with New Year's Eve. I misplace things, like New Year's Day. January 1st is always an awkward day. Every year there's at least two dozen sheepish-looking people with hangovers downtown, trying to find where they parked the car. I used to call my car Old Acquaintance because every New Year's Eve I forgot where I parked it.

With all the eating and guzzling, New Year's Eve is when you appreciate the truly thoughtful hostess. The one who puts bicarbonate in the cheese dip. I'm a conservative. When I go to one of those New Year's Eve parties where you have to bring a bottle, mine is aspirin.

Anything goes on New Year's Eve. I won't say how much kissing goes on at midnight, but at ll:55 there's a coast to coast run on Sen-Sen. And everybody cries a little. I think it's from throwing away that *Playboy* calendar. Can't you see Antony turning to Cleopatra on New Year's Eve and saying, "Just think, in fifteen seconds it'll be 32 B.C.!"

Once upon a time, this fellow went to a New Year's Eve costume party by himself because his wife wasn't feeling well. He met a mysterious masked woman. He wined her; he dined her; he danced with her; he romanced with her; he suggested they run away to Las Vegas for the weekend. And just then it was midnight. He pulled off his mask. She pulled off her mask--and it was his wife! And they both laughed--once upon a time.

New Year's Eve always seems to follow a pattern. Across the country, a 100 million people are watching their clocks, and 50,000 nightclub owners are watching their bartenders. One club owner calls his cash register The Punchbowl--'cause everybody keeps dipping in.

New Year's Eve is when millions of people celebrate Goliath style. They go out and get stoned. Last year I saw a guy try to drink champagne from a girl's shoe. It was

awful. It was a sandal. He'd been drinking bridge table whiskey. Three drinks and his legs folded up under him.

Last year a drunk boarded a bus, staggered up the aisle, flopped into a seat beside a little old lady. She looked him up and down, sniffed and said, "I've got news for you. You're going straight to hell!" The drunk jumped up and said, "Good heavens, I'm on the wrong bus!"

Driving a car on New Year's Eve is like playing Russian roulette. You never know which driver is loaded. The police have asked for our help in their drive against excessive New Year's drinking. So on December 31st they're planning to paint a thin white line down the center of all the dance floors and anyone who trips over the line--no more booze!

They say that gasoline and alcohol don't mix. Actually gasoline and alcohol do mix. It's just that the olives get stuck in the carburetor. On New Year's Eve you must be careful of icy roads. At this time of the year you can get 20 miles to the gallon when your foot is on the brake.

## *October*

Doesn't October weather do something to you? The air is just alive with the smell of burning leaves, apple cider, and mothballs. October is Surprise Month, when you zip open the plastic bags, pull out the clothes, and see which worked--the moths or the mothballs. Everybody seems to get their clothes out at the same time. "Darling, you smell delicious tonight. Chanel No. 5?"--"No. Black Flag No. 9!"

Autumn is when every man in America gets dressed up and has that certain air about him.

My wife puts mothballs in everything. I can understand mothballs for sweaters, mothballs for jackets, mothballs for suits--but in jockey shorts? I put on a pair this morning and by the time I reached the living room I'd invented three new dance steps.

October is when you open your storage closet and find you have a religious wardrobe--Holey! Holey! Holey!

Between baseball, football, golf and tennis matches, October is the month husbands spend the greatest amount of time watching TV. So many sports events are being shown on TV. A sports announcer called up the Mayo Clinic and asked, "Doc, can a tongue get a hernia?" Fellas who sit with a six-pack in front of a TV set and watch two football games and a golf tourney bring something special into a home--divorce.

You can always tell when baseball season is over and the football season is starting. The guys doing the shaving commercials are much bigger. Football is a game in which 22 big, strong, healthy men run around like crazy for two hours--while 50,000 people who really need the exercise watch them.

Autumn is a beautiful time of the year--when the leaves are turning yellow and teachers aren't too confident either. It's the time when Mother Nature goes through a change of leaf. Leaves slowly turn from green to brown to litter. I don't care how beautiful they are. I still say the only man whoever enjoyed falling leaves was Adam. I don't want to criticize Mother Nature, but wouldn't it have been a lot smarter to have leaves fall up?

## *Office Parties*

Sometimes I wonder if office parties are planned so much for fun as revenge--they all seem to follow a pattern. Sandwiches and bosses both get cut up in little pieces.

But the boss always goes the whole route. Orders a medley of 45 sandwiches, six of which are eaten. But they never go to waste 'cause at the end of the party, everybody has a dog who loves delicatessen.

One thing common to all office parties is paper cups. And there is one thing common to all paper cups--they leak. I've spilled so much liquor on my tie they don't dry clean it any more. They distill it.

I don't know why people knock office parties. Anything that lets you eat, drink, and dissipate on company time can't be all bad.

But even office parties are changing. I went to one where a computer spent two hours telling me about its operation. The computer got drunk and tried to unfasten the electric typewriter's ribbon.

You can always tell the old hands at Christmas office parties. They're the ones who apologize on the way in.

And you hear such fascinating bits of conversation at office parties--like, "Where's the bookkeeper?"

"Didn't you hear? The boss accused him of stealing."

"Did he leave in a huff?"

"No. A Rolls-Royce."

The person you have to watch out for at office parties

is the eager beaver who doesn't drink. Sips ginger ale; calls it a highball; then stands watching--and remembering. If this is your assistant, fire him in the morning. Remember what happened to Trotsky!

## Open House

Mama and I were invited to a high society "open house." It was informal. I got to wear my own clothes. The ladies all wore cocktail dresses; some of them showed good taste and that wasn't all! I guess the thing cocktail dresses leave to your imagination is what makes them so expensive. You could look at some of the young girls and tell what kind of past they were going to have.

I like cocktail parties. People drink at these affairs so they won't have to eat on an empty stomach. The samples of food are always good. Mama goes 'round and 'round the table sampling every "appeteaser" that's put out. I can't balance a drink on one knee and a plate on the other. It's the only time I wish for a lap. I usually wind up setting my glass in a gob of chip dip and get all gooey. Then Mama gives me hell for licking my fingers. She says etiquette condemns eating with the fingers. I say, if food isn't clean enough to pick up with the fingers, it's not fit to eat.

People are fun to watch. Some people want to drink to forget. The only thing they forget is to stop drinking. They drink between drinks. They come to the party very optimistically and leave very misty optically.

It's not necessary to understand things to argue about

them at a cocktail party. There wasn't much to talk about at this party until some of the guests were gone. They became the life of the party. You can always tell who are friends at an elbow-bending session. They dislike the same people. It's easy to get a whole house full of people to be friendly. The hard part is to get the people to like one another.

Mama says I shouldn't be so critical. Here's her motto, "Hear no evil, see no evil, speak no evil--and you'll never be a success at a party!"

## *Outer Space*

Despite all the turmoil and distrust here on earth we're still trying to determine if there is life in outer space. A lot of space exploration would have come to a halt if one of those five-mile-wide craters on the moon had turned out to be a belly button!

Every time I see those pictures of the moonscape I think they must have the same gardener we have. Barren, desolate, no water, no vegetation--looks just like some retirement land we've seen in the Southwest.

We've spent a billion dollars to find out if there's any intelligent life on Mars. Of course there's intelligent life on Mars. You can tell by the fact they're not spending a billion dollars to find out about us.

I knew Venus was uninhabited the first time we sent a rocket past it. Nobody asked for foreign aid. The surface of Venus is supposed to be humid, steamy, and 800 degrees, which would be impossible for life as we know it. How are you going to get postage stamps to stick on the envelope?

Personally, I think we are being watched by people from outer space. I also think they're going to contact the responsible leaders of earth--just as soon as they can find one. Did you ever get the feeling that, when it comes to flying saucers, the Air Force makes up its denials six months in advance?

There's a theory that UFOs are caused by swamp gas. If this is true, can you imagine what this will do to science-fiction movies? How will it look for the Air Force to be fighting back with bicarbonate?

I've just figured out why those flying saucers don't stay too long. Maybe it's a seven-planet tour in 14 days. People ask, "If flying saucers are people from outer space, why don't they contact us?" Would you?

The space shuttle has made us rather nonchalant about space flights. Since NASA has developed returnable space craft, it will soon become known as taking the 9:04 out of Cape Canaveral. All they need is a screwdriver with a handle 5,000 miles long for fixing missiles with second stages that don't work.

## Peaks & Valiums

Remember when we used to be afraid of nightmares? Now it's scarier the rest of the time. The average family today has so many problems, soap operas watch *them!*

For example, take a look at fashions. The top designers in the world are vying with each other to put their name on the back seat of jeans. People are becoming more and more designer conscious. It won't be long until the KKK will be wearing designer sheets.

There are two things you should know about status jeans. Because of the tailoring, you should never put anything in your pocket. And because of the price, you won't have anything left to put in your pocket. Status jeans are so tight, Zero Population Growth is encouraging couples to get married in them. By the time they get them off, they're divorced.

Diet is another problem. "Thin is in"--it's so far "in" that girls are starving themselves just to look like models; some

of them look like model skeletons. Children of privilege in a land of plenty are suffering from an epidemic that is sweeping the nation--anorexia nervosa--self-induced starvation that can waste its victims to the point they resemble victims of Nazi concentration camps.

Let's say your jeans aren't causing you to have a ringing in your ears, and you haven't reached the point where you must sit on a pillow because there's no meat left on your rump. Then you can take a crack at the problems caused by video games.

Experts say too many hours in front of a video game can result in "arcade arthritis." A rheumatologist found at least 65 percent of players studied had blisters, calluses, joint pain, or inflammation of a tendon as a result of repetitious manipulation of video game controls.

We wend our way through the peaks and valiums of life. It's fun trying to keep up with the Joneses, but every now and then couldn't they make a pit stop?

## *Picnics*

Folks used to cook indoors and go to the bathroom outdoors. Today all that has completely reversed. I've never completely adjusted to outdoor cuisine. One day I was operating a manual rotisserie, turning the crank round and round, barbecuing a chicken. A young man who watched from the sidewalk finally said: "I don't want to bug ya, dad--but your music's stopped and your monkey's on fire!"

As far as picnics are concerned, I think a picnic should

begin at noon and last 'til midnight; then you don't want any more picnics for a year, if ever. The more the mosquitoes, the better the picnic grounds; 50 million insects can't be wrong. Even though ants always seem to be at work, they still find time to go to picnics.

The picnic is distinctly an English institution. Up to recent times this outing-with-eats was a sparse and standardized affair consisting of ham or potted meat and sandwiches, and cold tea. We Americans could not leave well enough alone, so now come the well-filled hampers, portable coolers, portable stoves, plastic plates and spray-on bug killer.

I've never seen one of these mobile feasts with a "dietary department" observing at least the four most common dietary restrictions--no salt, no sugar, limited meat, low calorie intake. When the kitchen moves out to the hills, no holds are barred.

Honest-to-God outdoorsmen don't make a big deal out of hauling half the pantry to the hills. They tell me there are some 1,000 or more wild plants which botanists have reported to be safely edible. They can be prepared in many ways to yield complete meals. A possible dinner menu, for instance, might include a soup of day-lily flowers, main dish of sauteed giant puffballs with side dishes of bugleweed-root "potatoes" and pokeweed "asparagus", salad of ostrich ferns, bread from cattail pollen, beechnut coffee, and pineseed pudding for desert. Now, that's a picnic for you!

Personally, I'd just as soon not worry about my prospective dinner eating me.

# *Politics*

Politics are the only well-oiled machine that develops friction. If the Democratic candidate and the Republican candidate were each as unqualified and incapable as their opponents claim, the country would be in terrible shape no matter who got elected.

Politics is no place for the thin-skinned man. He's skinned too frequently. He must divide his time between running for office and running for cover. The word "politician" has acquired a sinister connotation because it is so often used by politicians to describe their opponents.

There are two sides to every question, and a good many politicians take both. If you think politics is easy, try standing on a fence while you keep your ear to the ground, and it's easy to distinguish a liberal in politics. He's the guy who wants to spend the conservative's money.

The two political parties may not love each other, but they sure don't want a third party. The impression grows that men who are mad enough to want to form a third party would make it two too many.

One of the problems with our government can be understood when we consider a remark made by an observer who had visited the United States Congress. He complained that the trouble with the government as he saw it was that there were too many Republican senators and too many Democratic senators and not enough United States Senators. The candidate who is seeking public office should dedicate himself to the interests of the country and the welfare of all the people instead of seeking to serve only a political organization and the voters of a party group.

The endless arguments in politics seem to be getting us nowhere. Right now we're in the same position as the pilot in a jet which was caught in a storm over Africa without a navigator. One of the staff asked the pilot how things were going, and he replied, "We aren't getting anywhere, but we certainly are making good time."

After watching some of our presidential hopefuls on TV, I was trying to explain to a European visitor how our American political system works. I said, "First, a candidate throws his hat into the ring." She said, "In Spain they put the bull in the ring." I said, "Same thing."

It's interesting to watch the aspirants and the half-aspirants vie for position. One politician has been a candidate so long he has orthopedic promises. He says his campaign is picking up speed. Isn't that what happens when you're going downhill? He's drawing such small crowds, he is beginning to whistle-stop. If anybody whistles, he stops.

It's an unfortunate thing, but even the candidates can't stop truth decay. I can remember when America's favorite exercise was jogging up the street. Now it's running down the government.

## *Pollution*

I didn't realize how bad the smog was until they started making freeway signs in braille. I can remember when "Smoke Gets in Your Eyes" was a song instead of a weather report. Now there's a song dedicated to the smog, "When Your Hair Has Turned to Silver and Your Eyes Have Turned to Red."

Air pollution is a little different from weather. Everybody talks about it, and everybody does something about it. They contribute to it!

However, there's one culprit that is beyond reproach-- and certainly beyond legislative control--Mother Nature!

Remember when we were so concerned about polluting the stratosphere that we banned aerosol products? Boom! Mother Nature started spewing volcanic ash from all directions, repelling sunlight and causing temperature inversions.

It's time the EPA rallied support of the demonstrators against volcano eruptions. "Hell No--Don't Blow!" would be a good battle cry. Or they could sit atop Mount St. Helens and sing, "We Will Be Overcome."

El Chichon, the fiery Mexican volcano, has shot 10 million tons of sunlight repelling ash and sulfur into the atmosphere covering most of North America. Talk about Montezuma's Revenge! We love those gorgeous sunsets, but there is a limit!

Surely we can spend a few billion bucks figuring out a method of corking those craters that insist upon undoing all the good things we have done. We agree that mankind is polluting everything he touches--but we aren't getting a whole lot of help from upstairs right now.

Of course, nature knows what she's doing, but sometimes it looks as if she organized mankind for the benefit of allergists and lung specialists. If nature is so wonderful, then why didn't she make the mosquito a vegetarian?

Nature is stubborn and will doubtless continue the policy of evolution, even though people get mad about it. Meanwhile, instead of putting anti-smog devices on cars, why don't they just put Murine in the gas. Or how about Hertz Rent-A-Lung?

## *Postal Rates*

The Postmaster General is proposing another increase in the price of first class stamps.

Those new rates will make stamp collectors out of millions of Americans--every time they want a stamp, they'll have to take up a collection. When you pay today's price for a stamp, and you start a letter with "Dear," you'd better believe it!

The increase will make it possible for the Post Office to use highly sophisticated electronic equipment. Instead of a $333-a-week clerk, your letters will be lost by a $20 million computer. At these rates they should put bourbon in the glue.

I love to go to the post office around Christmas time.

It's such a thrill watching them demolish a package just by stamping it FRAGILE. I don't want to put down the mail service, but if you really want to find out if a toy is unbreakable, send it parcel post. I know a woman who sent her son a Bible by parcel post. By the time it got to him, six of the Ten Commandments were broken. But you have to admit they are honest. I took a package to the Post Office and I said to the clerk, "It's rare imported crystal." He said, "Oh, was it?"

And they're having problems with deliveries. I know a letter carrier whose wife is in her 14th month. I don't want to complain about the postoffice, but when was the last time you got a "Get Well" card while you were still sick? I guess the postage stamp is a bargain. Where else can you mail a letter and have a half a million people work eleven days to deliver it?

I sent a Christmas card to Hawaii. Put one stamp too many on it. They did the only fair thing under the circumstances. Delivered it to China! Somewhere along the Yangtze River, there's a Chinaman standing in a rice paddy wondering, "Who he? What's a Cool Yule?..." Someday history books might attribute World War III to this incident!

## *Pot, Coke, and Ice*

I don't understand pot and coke, the fashionable vices of the "new class." I grew up in the middle class. We smoked cigarettes and drank beer. I can relate to that. We used to say, "Wow! What a party--I threw up four times and never missed the basin!" Our folks didn't take too kindly to our parties. I recall one night my dad put me to bed in the garage, but I couldn't sleep with him revving the engine.

But we were never caught sitting on the curb trying to suck the lug nuts off the truck. Today's parties are different. Strange things happen. At Woodstock they started diseases modern medicine still can't cure.

I have a young friend of whom I'm suspicious. He has a twitch in both eyes. When talking with him I need a dramamine just to maintain eye contact. I don't dare push him. I fear he'll snap and trash the place. We've watched him grow up. Now he's in college. He's taking political science and business, because he thinks some day he'd like to own his own country. He's planning to join a terrorist group just for the social life. He's going nowhere and his brain is making sure he gets there. When he graduates and gets his diploma he will do just as well with tea leaves.

He's had some interesting jobs. For a while he worked as a chicken dangler at a pit-bull fight and now he's filling condom machines in high school rest rooms. He also is a dishwasher at the college dorm.

He walks with a rhythmic jerk that seems to come from all that sound equipment he wears on his head--wires and tubes that look like an enema gone wrong. Fortunately we can't hear what's booming into his brain, but he seems to be going through constant changes. This month he dresses like a Viking.

He drives an old car that carries a bumper sticker: "GUNS DON'T KILL PEOPLE--I DO!" And he ties pieces of clothing to the front bumper. He gets the right-of-way! Are we seeing the building of a mass murderer from the ground up? He doesn't wear a seat belt because he says he "wants to be thrown clear!"

I'm not saying he's a "user", but strange things seem to happen when he's around. Once he tried to get the "wave" started at a funeral. Last year he told me about visiting the college band practice. While there he needed to go to the rest room. After wandering all over the music building he finally found the place. "I'll never forget," he said. "There was a gold toilet seat!" They're still trying to find the guy who ruined the tuba.

He doesn't have a steady girl friend. He once had a relationship that lasted 14 days. Then she chewed through the ropes and set herself free. He talks to himself and claims he's hearing voices.

I have a question. Do you suppose my young friend possibly could be using one of those popular miracle drugs? Lately he made mention of ice, so I looked it up. After using it, you experience 24 hours of euphoria, followed by two days of psychotic episodes. He'd pretty well need a three-day weekend to enjoy that stuff. Or, maybe he just grew up too near a breeder reactor.

I'd rather be drinking beer and hugging the toilet bowl. People like him are liable to make me pro-nuclear.

## *Prosperity*

If burning credit-card gas in installment cars over bond-built highways is prosperity, this country is still pretty doggone prosperous; but it is becoming quite evident that prosperity was the period when people ran up bills that are worrying them during a business recession. Prosperity? We Americans are the few people in the world who have to ask,

"How can I lose weight?" and "Where can I park?"

One test of prosperity is that you can always get credit enough to live beyond your means; you're paying installments on ten things instead of one. It's often the mink in the closet that is responsible for the wolf at the door.

Only Americans have mastered the art of being prosperous though broke. A typical American is someone who makes the down payment on a car for its clean, sleek lines--and then puts a ski rack in back and 500 pounds of camping equipment on top.

We have a warped idea of the necessities of life. This is a great age of convenience. We get our food in frozen packages, sermons by television, and babies by test tube. Progress has made it possible to go to the supermarket to get indigestion and a remedy for it at the same store. It will be 50 years before the human brain catches up with modern progress; and the worst of it is by the time we know where we are, we'll be somewhere else.

All we need to do is figure out how to pay for today's living. Even our politicians have arrangements whereby they can spend taxes before they collect them, but more and more people are beginning to doubt the more the country owes, the more prosperous it will be.

We are told, "To maintain our great national prosperity we must continue to spend. To insure our individual prosperity we must save." That clears that up!

"The only sensible road to prosperity is to live within our income," says an editorial. But few of us would care to be such misers.

I'm convinced that prosperity is something businessmen create and politicians take credit for it.

# Psycho-analysis

Did you ever get the feeling that life has put you on hold? Sometimes I think the winds of change have turned into a hurricane. If the world changes any faster, pretty soon the good old days will be 2:00 p.m.

They say, "Life is a cabaret"--and as you grow older you spend more time in the washroom. One of the great truths I've discovered is that the world isn't waiting for the sunrise. The only ones waiting for the sunrise are night watchmen.

I debated a long time before I went to see a psychiatrist. Personally I always tell my troubles to my enemies. They're the only ones who really want to hear them.

Psychoanalysis is when you pay $80 an hour to talk to a ceiling. I told him I felt like I was starting off on the wrong foot--and I'm a centipede. My life is a violin solo and I'm wearing mittens. Things just don't make sense to me any more, like playing strip solitaire.

He said, "It's all right to wrestle with your conscience, but don't make it two falls out of three." Then he threw those big words at me and said I was suffering from a "Cashew-Maraschino Syndrome." I said, "What's that?" He said, "Nutty as a fruit cake!"

Psychiatrists today have highly advanced techniques like group therapy. That's the psychiatrist's answer to automation. Group therapy is where ten people get together to solve their own problems--and at $30 apiece, the psychiatrist's problem too. One fella in our group said he doesn't care if his wife thinks she's an octopus, but it's costing him a fortune in elbow-length gloves. Another guy was really worried about his wife because she had posed for a nude picture. We told him he shouldn't worry about that. It's probably just an expression of her interest in art and asked what the nude photo was for. He said, "Her driver's license!"

It was an interesting experience. After the psychiatrist ushered out his last patient for the day, he heaved a weary sigh of relief, locked his door, turned on his hearing aid, and went home.

## *Recycled Star Dust*

Holy smoke! The whole world is coming apart! The earth's thermostat has blown a gasket, the ozone layer has a puncture, sunspots are going crazy and may knock out your TV, and one day last year every person on earth was bombarded with 10,000 billion neutrinos hurled into space by the explosion of a star. And that's just for starters.

I'm getting a little worried about this scientific rat race. I don't know if I'm slowing down or they're bringing in faster rats. I no longer have any incentive to buy a two-pants suit and I'm no longer clipping coupons. I even had a dream the flag we planted on the moon had shredded.

What the hell is a neutrino? It sounds like something cooked up by a Madison Avenue advertising agency, but how can they stick a label on an invisible object? Star gazers say these ghostly remnants of exploding stars are so incredibly small and elusive that they pass through buildings, people, and earth itself with barely a trace. How will we, the people, know they were here? When the first robin of spring falls out of a tree? Or when our tires start wearing from the inside out?

My God. Now we are recycled star dust! That mega-dose may explain why our kids are coloring the pictures in the sex manual and playing strip hopscotch. We're even planning an orgy at the Senior Citizen's Center. We're all going to take a big dose of barium and get together for a group X-ray. That should light up the place; we're the original star dust kids.

I've been wondering. If those neutrino things are so damned small, how did the whiz kids know we'd been zapped? They say they found traces in two huge vats of water, one in the U.S. and one in Japan. We're lucky those guys weren't around to test the water years ago when I was a kid taking Saturday night baths.

Being bombarded with 10,000 billion neutrinos some-how upsets me. That's a bunch of star dust. I'd rather have been revitalized by a shower of Neutrogena shampoo. I never figured to burn out before my picture tube did.

Not to worry, they say. People are constantly being showered with neutrinos from our own sun and the added dose did no harm. That's a refreshing bit of news, but I can remember when scientists spent all their time trying to figure out how old the earth is. Now they're just wondering how much older it's going to get.

Give me the days of the dinosaurs. Those were the days of achievement. The guys who hunted them not only had to set up decoys that weighed three tons, but they, too, were being constantly sand-blasted by exploding stars all around them. So what's new?

## Research

They did it again, didn't they? The medical researchers. They did it again. "Coffee Study Brews Cholesterol Threat," the front page headline blared.

Didn't we have this straightened out a long time ago? Weren't there studies showing caffeine to be bad? And other studies showing caffeine not to be bad? And other studies showing decaf the safest way to go?

If medical researchers made up restaurant menus, they'd have the entrees in one column and the corresponding causes of death in another.

Now, I'm really confused about all this medical research. Today just having a body has become a maintenance hassle. I'll forget the whole thing and go back to my cheese-filled chocolate doughnuts with bologna in them.

And it's not only medical research that's blowing my mind. "Oxy-fuels" with names like Ethanol and MTBE are being sold at local gas stations. In New Mexico they should be selling Guacahol--that's unleaded gas made from Mexican food. That would go over big here. These are people who think professional wrestling is real.

I just can't seem to keep up with things. Now there's a scented toilet paper. That does nothing but confuse the dog. And there's a new pregnancy test called "First Response"--it should be called "Last Resort." Television commercials keep trying to sell us a caulking compound called yogurt. And we're all supposed to have a bunch of condoms around the house. What the hell? Those things are made out of latex. House paint is made out of latex. Why not just keep a gallon beside your bed? That ought to last all winter.

The TV guy asks if we have a problem with cat-box odor. Yes, we do--the problem is we don't have a cat! It's a dog-eat-dog world today and sometimes I feel like I'm wearing Milk Bone underwear. Some researchers are so concerned with confusion they've become the patron saints of silliness.

I've been searching for an organization to help me through this muddle. I looked into the Society for Eternal Living--but if you die, you're out. Then I joined Loneliness Anonymous, but I kept going into this big room and no one was there. I finally settled for Liars Anonymous. It was hard at first. It took me six months to find them--they kept changing the address. But now I think I'll be comfortable there. Most of the members are researchers.

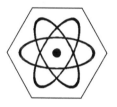

## *Science*

We just bought a microwave oven, and it's really great. It's the first time I ever got police calls on a roast beef. Scientists are now studying the effects of radiation from microwave ovens on human beings. The symptoms of over-exposure are headaches, fever, and the irresistible urge to sit in a bathtub full of gravy.

The contributions modern science has made to our lives are amazing. I bought six hot dogs that are so filled with chemicals, you have to cook them over a Bunson burner, and it's just fantastic what they're doing to bread these days. You can buy a loaf, put it on the shelf, and two weeks later it still will be fresh. However, it does have a tendency to develop a slow leak.

We have become victims of the hypnosis of science. Technicians are working to prolong life so we can have time to pay for all the gadgets they invent. But it seems science never solves a problem without creating ten more.

Now they're tinkering with the creation of artificial life, and we suppose before another decade the stork will be bringing 'em in cans.

Why don't they get down to the practicalities of life, like inventing a vaccination scar that would look like a dimple; or cigarette ashes which will match the color of the rug; or crossing a steel plant with a rubber plant so we could buy tires with metal rims?

In between figuring out ways to abolish sleep, and counting mosquitos eaten by fish, there's another crew constantly studying the evolution of man. One biologist suggests the American people walk on their four limbs in order to live longer. They'd live just long enough to get started across the street.

The bishop of London said that religion and science go hand-in-hand. They do, but every now and then one of them lets go and hands the other a nasty wallop.

One scientist suggested that man retained his tail sometime after he became intelligent. But then the earliest caves never had revolving doors. Another says that mankind is of vegetable origin. Obviously. Man descended from monkeys and monkeys came from trees.

Scientists say this universe is made up of protons, photons, electrons, and neutrons. They forgot to mention morons.

# *Sex*

"The biggest problem with the world today is sex. People are drenched in novels about sex, films about sex, lectures about sex. Advertising is based on sex. Schools have sex education courses. We're becoming obsessed with sex, sex, sex! Now, what do you say about that?"

"Your place or mine?"

It's amazing the way sex has dominated the American outlook. Take literature. There's "Sex and the Single Girl," "Sex and the Single Man." They even have a new football manual--"Sex and the Single Wing."

Sex in college has gotten so much publicity that all over the country schools are faced with a brand-new problem--drop-ins. It's called the free-sex movement, and so far the only thing that's right about it is the price. I'll say one thing for sex in college--at least parents know their kids are in bed by eleven. They don't know whose.

A lot of parents are worried for nothing. Yesterday I overheard this conversation between two college kids--and it was refreshing to hear how concerned they were over their studies:

"Sheila, I'm having a terrible time with my applied calculus. Do you think you could help me?"

"Of course I could help you, Stanley."

"Good. Your bed or mine?"

I don't know what's happening to kids, but the progressive school gives three tests a semester--a midterm, an end-term, and a Wasserman. You'd be surprised how many college kids are in their fourth year and six months. Girls are graduating magna cum pregnant. Some girls are graduating with an M.A.--and others as a MA! They say 45 percent of the colleges and universities are handing out birth control information. The rest are handing out diapers. One teenage mother is so young, when she called up the doctor about diaper rash, he said, "Whose?"

Teenagers have always had a sex drive, but years ago they occasionally put it in neutral. Personally, I don't think either side is going to win the Sexual Revolution. Too much fraternizing with the enemy!

## *Smoking*

Just when a lot of people are quitting smoking, scientists say breathing the air of any big city is like smoking two packs of cigarettes a day. I can just see the ads of the future, "I inhale Pittsburgh--it satisfies!"

I just figured out a way to really stop people from smoking. Don't tell 'em it's unhealthy. Tell 'em it's fattening!

All kinds of crash programs exist to make people stop smoking. They've labeled every package of cigarettes, "Caution--Cigarette Smoking is A Health Hazard". Heck, so is marriage. Try coming home at three in the morning without an excuse.

The tobacco industry is hot water over all kinds of new ideas. They must make a profit to pay dividends to the American Medical Association stockholders. They even put charcoal in filter tips so you can smoke cigarettes and broil your nose at the same time. They're also experimenting to make a synthetic tobacco from vegetables. Can't you just see yourself going into a store and saying: Gimme a pack of asparagus--plain tip. And there's one consisting of nothing but lettuce. It won't have a filter--mayonnaise. Maybe they should take out your Adam's apple and put a filter in.

Believe me, it isn't as hard as you think to give up smoking. All you need is will power, determination, and wet matches. I know a lot of people who have sworn off. And the swearing doesn't stop there. They substitute other things. I won't say what, but some are buying bourbon in the handy sixpack. I saw one who substituted candy bars; he put a candy bar in his mouth without unwrapping it, lighted it and said, "Man, that's real chocolate!"

People who give up smoking have the same problem as people spending their first day at a nudist camp--what to do with their hands. I'll say one thing for smoking three packs a day. It gives your hands something to do--shake!

You know what could really start trouble--science discovering a definite link between cancer and sex! That's still unproven, but I think there can be no doubt left in anyone's mind, that smoking definitely causes reports.

## *Social Security*

Most Americans only ask one thing of Social Security: That when they reach 65, the government will support them as well as they've supported it.

Now they're talking about having Social Security begin at age 68--but to make up for it, they're going to include maternity benefits. One company is really going with the new, later retirement age. They've gone from: "Get Out Alive at 65" to "Vegetate til 68--Die on the Job!"

I'd feel a lot better about the bureaucrats who are fixing the Social Security system if they didn't fight so hard to keep from being under it themselves. You have to be a little suspicious of anyone who accompanies you to Lover's Leap but doesn't want to hold hands.

Taxation is now based on the same principle as that razor with two blades. The income tax takes most of what you have and Social Security takes what's left. It makes you wonder if there will be enough poverty around when you reach 65. When you look at your paycheck today you think they've finally nationalized mugging.

Social Security makes for a very logical sequence of events. To pay for it, all of our lives we have to work like a dog so that when we retire, we can eat Alpo.

I never really believed retired people were eating dog food until that poll came out. The one that lists their four favorite forms of recreation: golf, television, shuffleboard, and chasing cars. What kind of wine goes with Alpo?

Thanks to inflation, we can count on two things in our golden years--silver hair and a tin cup. In all fairness, the government does guarantee our Social Security. In the next decade the monthly check will just about keep you in Certs.

They tell us not to worry. If you're retired and you hear about Social Security going broke, don't worry. If you're retired and you read about Social Security paying out five billion dollars more than it is taking in, don't worry. But if you're retired and you notice your Social Security check is post-dated--worry!

## *Stinky, Clean Air*

After living together for 50 years, Madeline and I have developed a rather complete understanding of each other's peculiarities and mannerisms. We have become very sensitive to the other's intellectual senses, such as sight, hearing, and touch as well as corporeal senses of taste and smell. We know which colors, foods, music, and odors are preferred.

Odors can be a point of contention. Madeline doesn't enjoy the smell of lemon or garlic. I detest the smell of fish. I like the smell of toast and tobacco; she loves the fragrance of fruit odors and flowers. That gives me hay fever. We both try to stay away from nauseating odors.

Think about this. Wherever you go, whatever you do, there's an odor connected with it, whether it's new mown hay or carbon monoxide; a bowl of chili or turtle soup. It has always been true.

When we were kids the streets smelled like horse manure--you think that's bad? Just take a deep breath today in Downtown Anywhere. Horse droppings smell like daisies in comparison and it's not getting any better.

For the past year or so, there's been a new nasty auto odor causing some concern in our marital relations. It seems every time we've been stopped at a busy intersection, the "go" light causes an "outhouse" odor to float through our car.

Madeline gives me a look of uncertainty and asks, "Did you....?"

I always firmly interrupt, "No--there must be a sewage

treatment plant around here."

This has been going on for a couple of years. She knows me better than that. When I do a "did you..." the sense of hearing comes into use before the olfactory nerve goes to work. In fact, long ago I classified "did you..." into four categories: "fuzz" -- "fizz-fuzz" -- "pooper" -- and "rattler". I've developed the "rattler" into an art form. To me "did you..." is not an idiosyncrasy, it's a necessity. I am no longer in the "fuzz" stage. She knows that.

Why me? Why do I always have to be the one to think up the answers, such as "someone forgot to put lime in the two-holer" --or "lightning must have hit the septic tank"

Lately the questioning has become more intense. "Are you *sure*. Did you...?"

I've started firing back. "I'm telling you once and for all-- *I don't* do the 'did you' every time a traffic light turns green! Did YOU?"

That return question gets her going with a quick little jerk of the head as though suddenly she has seen something fly past her window.

Sooner or later this nasty odor would have gotten to more than our noses. There's too much traffic and too many signal lights to maintain the peace.

So, I developed a new answer: "Hell, yes! Gotta Tum or two?" This was a solution. She *always* carries Tums, and always eagerly shares them. The situation reached the point when El Stinko seeped into the car, Madeline just quietly handed me a roll of Tums. Discussion ended.

The other day, while reading the morning paper, Madeline looked up and asked, "Do you remember when the entire high school knew you were making rotten-egg gas?"

Now there's a trick question if I ever heard one. It wasn't just Old Jack that was making rotten-egg gas. It was part of the demonstrations in Chemistry class. Even the teacher was in on the trick. It was called H2S--hydrogen sulfide.

"Why do you ask? Someone else cause a high school holiday?"

"No," she said, "but, it says here that the new cars have a three-way catalytic converter that converts harmful emissions into hydrogen sulfide, or H2S. It also says a lot of people have been complaining about a nasty odor, and it seems to be most prevalent immediately after full throttle accelerations.

"For the most part this nasty odor did not exist with older two-way converters, but became common with the introduction of three-way converters--did you...know that?"

Voila! John King, manager of the service engineering office at Ford Motor Co.'s parts and service division, has vindicated me! He says all gasolines have some sulfur which undergoes a chemical reaction in the catalytic converter. The H2S odor comes from the new third stage when nitrous oxides are treated.

Aha--do you want polluted air, or stinky clean air?

Thank you, Mr. King, for making the next 50 years of our marriage a bit more calm, even though Norcliff Thayer, Inc., Tarrytown, N.Y. is probably wondering why there's been a decline in the sale of Tums.

## *Stress*

Today we're experiencing anxieties people never even dreamed of twenty years ago. Everybody's feeling guilty about something. People are so nervous the newest calorie books give the count for fingernails. I wouldn't say I'm nervous. It's just that the butterflies in my stomach are like the Strategic Air Command--flying at all times.

Right now, things are so confused, I know a Ouija Board that just shrugs. I won't say how insecure people are getting, but Dial-A-Prayer just added two more numbers. Personally, I never have any problems in coping with the realities of life. I just follow those four magic words a wise old Indian guru once taught me: "When In Doubt--Crumble!"

Everybody's shook up these days. Teenagers are upset because they're living in a world dominated by nuclear weapons--and adults are upset because they're living in a world dominated by teenagers.

You know what our big problem is? We've run out of slogans. "Remember The Alamo!" "Remember The Maine!" "Remember Pearl Harbor!" What do we have to remember today? Our ZIP code! People are so confused these days, you'd be surprised how many people get in a cab and give the driver their ZIP code. I'm so weary. They expect me to remember my ZIP code, my area code, my phone number, my social security number, my bank account number. Are they kidding? I still write 1989 on checks! I've made it a point to memorize my credit card numbers--if for no other reason than I don't like my wallet knowing more than I do.

Today's youngsters have found a way to cope with anxiety. They sing about it! I don't want to panic anybody, but three million electric guitars with amplifiers were given out as Christmas presents last year. This could be the end of eardrums as we know them. It's really amazing the way the guitar has dominated the world of music. When I was a kid--with Roy Rogers and Gene Autry--we never thought of a guitar as an instrument. It was more like a weapon. The way things are going, the world won't end with a whimper, but with a twang!

## *Sunday School*

Some little kids attend church like they're being held hostage. In the middle of a sermon, one youngster leaned over and whispered to his mother, "Mom, if we give him the money now, do you think he'll let us go?"

The kids like the music, but the commercials are too long. They're geared to modern times. They expect Moses to come down from Mount Sinai, read the Ten Commandments from a paperback and then say, "Coming up next, sports and the weather!"

One little lad went home from Sunday School and proceeded to tell his mother all about Moses and the Red Sea crossing. "Moses got behind the enemy lines," the youngster said, "and he had his engineers build a pontoon bridge. Moses and his people then crossed over. When his spies told him a corps of Egyptian tanks was about to cross the bridge, he got on his walkie talkie and ordered his Air Force to blow up the bridge. The Air Force blew it up and the Israelites were saved." "Did the Sunday School teacher tell you the story just like that?" the mother asked. "No," he said, "but the way she told it, you wouldn't believe it!"

Fifteen-year-old Todd had volunteered to teach a Sunday School class for four-year-olds. When asked what he had scheduled for the first lesson, he replied, "Well, the lesson plan says, 'Show them that each person has different potentialities and abilities, each is valuable for these capabilities, differences outweigh conformity.'"

"If that doesn't work," he said, "we'll make clay bunnies."

Little girls also are a problem. They've heard so much about equal rights that they want to hear the gospel according to Matthew, Mark, Luke, and Shirley.

The more I see of kids, the more I'm coming to the conclusion I was never their age. I had very understanding parents. I'll never forget the time I told them I was into atheism. They said, "All right, just so long as you clean up your room afterwards!"

Back in those days we had permanent diapers and disposable kids!

## Teenage Fathers

There's big news today! The National Institute of Child

Health and Human Development has been funded for a study of teenage fathers. The study is funded by the Federal Office of Population Affairs and the William T. Grant Foundation.

Teenage fathers? I didn't know there were any. We've seen plenty of publicity about teenage mothers and teenage pregnancy. But, teenage fathers? Where have they been hiding these kids?

There weren't any teenage fathers when I was a kid. Well, maybe one or two. When I was growing up nobody seemed to know just who it was that "fixed" the girl. Keeping it a secret was a matter of life or death.

There was one teenage marriage in our high school. The parents were part of the upper crust in our small town society. I remember when the father of the bride came into our printing office to order wedding announcements. Dad Lacy asked him, "Where was your son-in-law when you first met him?" The father of the bride replied, "Right smack in the middle of my shot gun sights."

Teenagers were the same then as now. The same juices have always been flowing. We weren't shy--we were scared! Girls were well protected. The two guards we feared most were Mr. Colt and Mr. Remington. In those days gun control was being able to hit your target.

We all knew that girls matured more quickly than boys. Girls' maturity was more obvious. We could look at a girl and couldn't help but think that under her coat, her sweater, her dress, her slip--that girl was stark naked! We were smart enough to know that cleavage wasn't something butchers did.

From that point forward it was just a matter of whether or not we were willing to stake our lives on that magnetic attraction.

Serving as head honcho of the Pep Squad when I was a senior offered a great opportunity to judge the maturity of new quail in the high school freshman class. Freshman girls liked senior boys. Senior girls were getting sex education from various and sundry graduates.

I recall one voluptuous little freshman girl who joined the cheerleaders. When she donned that little skirt with "cross-your-heart" suspenders, she really showed off her pom-poms. She jumped in double-time.

One evening I walked her home from school. We sat on the porch swing and enjoyed small talk, including a date for the next evening when I would buy her an ice cream soda on the walk from school.

When we approached her home on that memorable second date we spotted her father sitting on the porch swing. "I wonder what he is doing home so early?" questioned little Josephine.

As we walked up their front sidewalk we could see that double-barrel shotgun beside him on the swing.

"I think it's time for you to leave," she said. (My God, how many times have I heard that?)

"Yeah. See you later." I didn't even "howdy" with her Dad. I never went back!

This type of family introduction had a tendency to hold down the rate of teenage pregnancies.

Courting your girl on a bicycle wasn't too much fun. There weren't many cars. You either rode a bike to school or you walked. However, if you really wanted to ruin some Romeo's love life, it was easy. Just steal a brassiere from your sister's dresser drawer, take it to the school bike rack and stretch it across the handle bars. Word spread like wild-fire, not only through the school, but the whole town. From then on that kid was dead in the water.

It was more fun to walk your girl home from school, even if you had to push your bike. You could leave your bike on the lawn and sit with her on the porch swing. Every home had a porch swing. These "two seater" jobs were hung by chains to the porch ceiling. The chains were never lubricated. They were supposed to squeak like hell. That sound kept her folks informed whether or not you were swinging. You *never* just sat in a swing.

Girls were professional porch-swingers. At night the swings were great. Girls knew how to cuddle up, tuck their legs up in the swing and the guy knew how to keep the chains squeaking.

On a warm summer night there you were, making love in a swing while her folks were inside the screen door listening to Amos and Andy on the radio. But the folks kept the radio tuned low to make sure they didn't miss a squeak on the front porch.

Girls didn't get pregnant in a porch swing, but the boys sure learned how to do touchy-poo while rattling the chains.

I sat in dozens of porch swings and only let one stop-- maybe for five minutes. Everything was pleasingly peaceful as we cuddled on that swing--then, Blam! The front door screen flew open and her father hit the porch on the dead run. He looked me squarely in the eyes and said, "Oh! I thought you'd gone home--I just came out for some air."

"I think it's time for you to leave," she said.

"Yeah. See you later." There's nothing more dangerous than a breathless father.

One thing about it, we didn't suffer from the maladies that plague today's kids. There were no stiff wrists from turning knobs on video games, no Frisbee fingers, and we sure didn't suffer from "back pocket sciatic" caused by sitting on thick billfolds. We just suffered from motion sickness from those blasted swings, splinters in the elbow from reaching your arm across the back of the swing in order to get a better hold on things, and heart failure from those near-misses with protective papas.

Funny thing. After we were married, Madeline's folks dismantled the swing, got rid of the dog, put away the rifle and went inside to watch Milton Berle on their black-and-white TV.

Times change everything; but why should we spend a couple of million bucks studying teenage fathers when all we need to do is take away the folks' TV, sell the car, put up a porch swing, and buy a shot gun.

ENTERTAINMENT

## *Television*

You know what I like about watching television? The commercials! According to them the biggest problem facing America today is bad breath. I know a guy who's so impressed by that bad-breath commercial, every time he goes into a drug store to buy the product, he's afraid to open his mouth.

The commercial that always shakes me is the one about rough, red hands. It makes you sound like a Communist dishwasher. And commercials are now so loud, if you go to the bathroom during one, it comes right in with you. They'll tell you how to get rid of a headache in 60 seconds, but it comes on so loud, it gives you another one.

The toothpaste ads are really interesting. I understand the group that had 21 percent more cavities also had 38 percent more pregnancies. You see, without brushing they had all this time on their hands. I often wonder if the kids who have 34 percent more cavities could sue?

Since watching TV commercials I've found out all about the lower digestive tract. They give all these things very dignified, high-falutin' names, like hypertensive gastric acidity. Ten syllables just to say, "burp." I always thought irregularity was someone who came in to work late; thanks to TV, I know better.

People never used to talk about armpits until television came along. Now, thanks to commercials, it's as acceptable a subject as irregularity, slipping dentures, or postnasal drip. I don't have anything against underarm deodorants. I just think there's something morally wrong in having my armpits smell better than the rest of me.

These commercials really get to people. I know a fella who's obsessed with the idea of not offending. Every morning he gets up, takes a shower with deodorant soap, washes his hair with dandruff remover, brushes his teeth with a breath sweetening toothpaste, gargles with a germicide, drains his sinus cavities, closes his pores, squirts spray deodorant over his cream deodorant, and this man has never offended! How can he? He never gets out of the bathroom!

I'm just amazed at some of the things they're selling on TV--like lemon rinse. I guess it's for people who have the uncontrollable urge to rinse lemons.

There is a lot of creativity in TV. Do you think it's easy making a 20-second commercial seem like a full minute? If the commercial proves to be embarrassing, it seems to last longer than a minute. For instance, we didn't know that women suffered from feminine itching and irritation until the medicated, disposable douche came on TV.

Now that women have become liberated, the girls have no secrets. Everyone knows about their panty shields, Maxi Pads (super, regular and deodorant) and tampons. The advertisers must think the menstrual cycle comes every thirty days and lasts a month. For the first time in history feminine hygiene has become a spectator sport--along with indigestion and bad breath.

I love to watch late night TV, with all those wonderful old movies and variety acts. In the thirties, you could see two of these movies for a dime. Now it costs you $900 for a TV set and what do you see? Those same movies.

During the thirties Jimmy Cagney was the toughest guy in the movies. Remember Jimmy Cagney? He was sort of a bonsai John Wayne. In the thirties they also made those spectacular pictures with hundreds of beautiful dancing girls covered with glitter. Some of these girls were so loaded with glitter the actors didn't know whether to kiss them or pawn them. I was 18 before I realized show girls didn't grow sequins. And tap-dancing was very big. Every movie had eight big production numbers; eight incredible sets; eight lavish costume changes; and, one time step. One actress got to be a star because she had three variations on the time step: slow, fast, and uncertain. Back in those days they spent so much money to buy stars, sets, costumes, and 10,000 extras, they didn't have anything left for a plot.

The great biblical epics followed. Some of them were so long they were a spectacle for the eyes, a revelation for the ears, and a challenge for the kidneys. And such great scenes! Noah putting two of everything on the ark. Two of everything! I think it was a government job. I can see him now, standing at the gangplank of the ark as two of everything went marching by: "There are two elephants. Two lions. Two tigers. Two leopards. Raquel Welch."

We saw Moses coming down from Mount Sinai. Coming down with two tablets and a hernia. Aren't you glad Moses isn't alive today? How would it sound, turning to his secretary and saying, "Take a Commandment!"

Remember all those great John Wayne westerns? This man had muscles like Jackie Gleason had chins. John always was standing at one end of main street with arms outstretched, ready to draw. Sometimes I wondered if he was sheriff or a test pilot for underarm deodorant. But things are changing. Hollywood is now making a western so modern, the Indian medicine man is a pediatrician!

However, we must give today's movie makers credit for an interesting rating system. If a movie is rated R, it means they can touch a woman's breast. If it's X-rated, they're allowed to cut it off with a chain saw.

## *Texas*

I don't care how much money you have--if you want to feel poor, go to a picnic in Texas. Even the paper plates are sterling!

I'm not knocking barbecue sauce, but in Texas, if you can taste the meat, someone goofed. Thanks to barbecue sauce, nobody needs to learn how to cook in Texas. This stuff has covered up more mistakes than a maternity bridal gown. You order a sirloin and by the time they finish adding the sauce it looks like steak soup. Sometimes I wonder if they really like barbecue sauce or they're just hooked on Tums. The first time I tried Texas barbecue sauce I had an interesting experience. I spilled some on my shirt. That may not be interesting to you, but now I have two belly buttons.

We used to live in Texas so I feel free to explain a little about that great state. Texans love Texas stories and they have a million of them.

I know a Texan so rich, he bought a bomb shelter with a built-in house. All of his furniture is oily American. Even the kitchen has seven rooms and he has one of those

Texas bathrooms--where the sink has three faucets--hot, cold, and bourbon. He is a lazy Texan who bought his wife a yacht for Christmas--so he'd have nothing to wrap.

They do things big in Texas. They have an auto showroom in Dallas, three acres wide and wall-to-wall with Cadillacs, Lincolns, Imperials. Over in one corner, there's a pile of Volkswagens with a placecard, "Take One." One Texan is so rich he doesn't have his Cadillac air-conditioned. Just keeps a half-dozen cold ones in the freezer. There's an antique car club in Dallas restricted to owners of Cadillacs no longer under the new car guarantee.

My idea of real living is that big Texas family with six sports cars to run around the ranch. Twice a year, they send the foreman out in a Cadillac to round them up.

A highly unreliable source informs us of the fella who dies, goes to heaven, and is strolling down the streets of gold, listening to the angelic music--when suddenly he sees a column of men, trudging along in chains. Shocked to the core, he runs to St Peter and asks, "Prisoners? Prisoners in heaven?" And St. Peter nods his head sadly and answers, "Texans. They keep trying to get back."

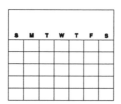

## Thanksgiving

Inviting your relatives for Thanksgiving dinner performs a useful function. It eliminates loneliness, quiet, and leftovers.

The average mother takes two whole days to prepare

Thanksgiving dinner, but most kids don't care. If Twinkies came with drumsticks, all turkeys would die of old age.

When I was a kid, we were so poor our Thanksgiving dinners were a little different from most. We started off with leftovers. Inflation may put a crimp in the festive board this year. Some people are getting desperate; I just saw a magazine article, "How to Stuff a Drumstick!"

Thanksgiving is a great time for families to get together. Scarcely any heritage is comparable to that of having deeply seeded into one's childhood the joys, companionship, and ecstacies of a happy family having fun together.

In an essay on "Things I am Thankful For," a little boy listed "my glasses." He explained, "They keep the boys from fighting me, and the girls from kissing me."

Everybody was thankful at the first Thanksgiving. The Pilgrims were thankful they had landed safely in the New World--and the Indians were thankful they hadn't landed 200 years earlier. Frankly, if I had been an Indian, I'd have wished Plymouth Rock had landed on the Pilgrims.

I've always been fascinated by those guns the Pilgrims carried--with the wide muzzle. I never knew if it was a gun or a .45 caliber plunger. Incidentally, the history books are wrong about one thing. They claim the turkey the Pilgrims roasted on that first Thanksgiving was wild. This is only half true. He was not wild until he found out what they had in mind!

Nowadays all you can buy is frozen turkeys. Turkeys are so frozen that they enjoy the first three hours in the oven. After one Thanksgiving dinner I asked my wife, "Is this a frozen turkey?" She said, "Yes." I said, "My compliments to the refrigerator." I didn't want to say anything at the time, but I think we ate a sick turkey. All afternoon it had a thermometer in it.

The Russians put out a news report that things are so bad in this country that on Thanksgiving Day a hundred million Americans will be eating stale scraps of bread--and they will be. It's called stuffing. Thanksgiving is the day when millions of Americans finally do something about their weight. Increase it!

Learning to cook a turkey takes years of experience. When we were first married, and my wife took the turkey out of the oven and removed the aluminum foil, she was throwing away the best part. I remember asking her, "Where did you get this recipe?" She said, "It's a very good recipe. I got it out of a magazine." I asked, "Which one? *Popular Mechanics?*"

My neighbor has an interesting theory about Thanksgiving. He feels most families have so many relatives coming for Thanksgiving dinner, they'll never notice one more. So, for the last ten years he's been going into some strange house on Thanksgiving Day and saying he's Uncle Harry. Nine times it worked out well, the tenth time it worked out great. There was another phony claiming she was Aunt Harriet and they put them up for the night.

Some people get squeamish about raising their own turkey for Thanksgiving, but not me. One year we bought a live turkey in January. We called him Clarence and all through the year we fed him, took him for walks, played with him. He was just like one of the family. But when it came November there was no nonsense about it. We had him for Thanksgiving dinner. Clarence sat on my right.

I have to admit I have a terrible time carving turkey. I'll tell you how bad it is--one year the turkey's family sued for malpractice. I'm one of those nervous carvers. I shake so much, each year we have an etiquette problem. What wine goes with fingers? Every year around Thanksgiving and Christmas you see helpful articles on "How to Carve a Turkey." They're really practical. Now all I need to find is a butcher who sells those turkeys with dotted lines.

The week after Thanksgiving you sit down to dinner

and ask, "Are we have pheasant under glass?" and your wife answers, "No. We're having turkey under Saran wrap!"

It's the same thing every year. First you have roast turkey. Then the next day you have warmed-up turkey, followed by cold turkey, followed by turkey croquettes, followed by turkey omelette, followed by turkey hash, followed by turkey soup, followed by Christmas.

## *Travel Tours*

Today the big travel gimmick is tours that cover 12 countries in 21 days. This is like reading every 50th word in the *Encyclopedia Britannica*--you're moving so fast, by the time you look in your guidebook to see where you are--you ain't. One tour goes to seven countries in two weeks. What can you see in two weeks? It's like reading *Playboy* with your wife turning the pages.

Thanks to modern jet air travel, now we can be sick in countries we never heard of before. Did you ever get the impression some of these countries try to qualify as a tourist paradise by importing their water from Mexico?

Last year we took one of those Dysentery Tours--14 bathrooms in 7 days. Someone asked me, "Did you see the fountains of Rome?" I said, "If it flushed, I saw it!" My big problem was the tour guide. Every day we stopped in 22 souvenir shops and one restroom. Naturally. Who gets kickbacks from rest rooms? Tour guides are big for tips. These people can clear their throats in 15 languages.

If you are planning one of these tours, let me give you my recipe for the perfect martini. Three parts gin to one part Kaopectate.

Many European resorts are set up with one bath, and you share it. Sometimes with two other hotels. Naturally, this calls for some resourcefulness. My five-day deodorant pads were giving out in six hours and 42 minutes.

There's very little difference between the tourists of

today and the tourists of 25 years ago. They're still buying the Brooklyn Bridge only now they put it on the American Express card. Many of us wished we were as rich as the foreigners think we are.

Customs examiners are the only men I know who don't get excited by a 42-26-38 figure. Too often, the 42 is watches. One feminine traveler in our party had a problem: The customs officer asked, "Have you anything special to declare, madam?"

"No," she replied, "not a thing."

"Am I to understand, my lady," the officer replied, "that the fur tail hanging down under your coat is your own?"

## Tumbleweeds

Pity the poor tumbleweed. No state has adopted it as its State Flower. Everyone cusses it. The original prickly plague of the plains, its only contribution to American culture was Gene Autry's song, "Tumblin' Tumbleweeds", the tempo of which failed to match these bouncing balls.

Tumbleweeds come in four basic sizes: Flyers, Scooters, Bouncers, and Heavy Rollers.

Flyers: No larger than a dinner plate. This scrawny variety lacks the weight to stay on the ground and usually travels about windshield high. When the dust settles, you'll find them stuck in tree limbs, perched on roofs, or gracing the top of a flag pole.

Scooters: Too heavy to fly, too light to bounce or roll.

They normally scoot along on their butts. They're about the size of a kettle drum. This variety just scrapes and scoots along, dropping into ditches and stacking up against fences and buildings, forming the ramps and inclines for the heavy artillery as the forces invade.

Bouncers: This fast-mover is as big as a truck tire and jumps like a kangaroo. In a high wind you'll see it hit the ground, bounce into the air, travel in an arc for 100 yards, hit the ground and repeat the performance. It can jump fences, ditches, barns, and rivers.

Heavy Rollers: Range in size from a manhole cover to a horse tank. The heavy artillery of the invasion, they rumble across land with a terrifying force. They cross ditches filled by the advance guard and climb the ramps built by Scooters and Bouncers. They have been know to come to rest on top of barns, silos, and shopping centers.

All types are indestructible, built with a hobnail tread that enables them to move northward on a 50-mile-an-hour wind, travel 100 miles and reverse direction. Aside from scattering their trillions of seeds to reproduce more troops, the tumbleweeds, after years of back-and-forth maneuvers across the western plains, prairies, and towns, all receive the battle citations of various colors. The whites are rookies, browns, seasoned veterans. But the grays and blacks are the old soldiers that never die--they just blow away.

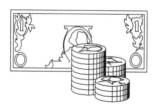

## U. S. Budget

Congress is hung up on the fiscal year's budget. Fiscal year--that's an accounting device that postpones bad news for six months. The debt limit is Government by American Express. If the meek inherit the earth any time soon, they'll inherit debt enough to keep them that way. The "passing generation" is so called because of the debts it is passing along to the next.

The difference between economy and extravagance is the difference between a Republican and a Democrat discussing the administration's appropriations. No matter what political platform is built, or who builds it, the economy plank always gets lost.

A Detroit congressman has an idea that will save us eight billion dollars in defense spending. We use last year's rockets, but we change the grille a little.

We don't mind supporting the government, but we think the government should leave us enough to support ourselves. Our government does not profess to live within its income, but only within ours. Our forefathers objected to taxation without representation. Now we would be glad to get taxation without misrepresentation.

Politicians seem to fall into two groups: Those that do their best and those that do their constituents. I know one politician who went to Washington to take the pulse of the nation--and anything else that wasn't nailed down.

The President is having the same problem with Congress I have with my wife. Always arguing about money. Personally, I don't have anything against the government wanting to fight poverty. It's just that they always want to use my savings as ammunition. Remember the good old days when a government handout was a politician offering to shake?

If the government is really looking for additional revenue, how about charging extra for low ZIP code numbers? Or put Medicare under the Department of

Agriculture so people would be paid for not growing an appendix. They could save seven billion dollars if they took Medicare out and put Christian Science in. There's so much cutting being done on the new budget the President will have to sign it with a styptic pencil.

I remember when we criticized the government for its extravagance in giving away free seeds. What people today crave is a government that will support and not tax them.

The average American believes in government by majority so long as the majority doesn't want something to which he objects. Today the majority gets at least two guesses as to which minority will rule them next.

No system of government will work in the land where everybody tries to work the government. All we want today is lower taxes and larger appropriations. No government can long exist with half the people supporting it and the other half holding it up.

## *Vacations*

A travel folder is a "trip tease;" after a while you learn to translate the jargon. "Conducive to complete relaxation" means the place is dead. "A charming atmosphere of rustic simplicity" means no inside plumbing. "Twenty-fifth season under the same owner-management" means they haven't been able to sell the place. "Bathing nearby" means the hotel has no swimming pool. "Spacious grounds--350 acres" means you've got to walk two miles from your cottage to the dining hall. Most people use this year's vacation to find out where to stay away from next year.

It's nice to get away from it all. It's a long-awaited rest, except for the pocketbook. The best place to spend your vacation is just inside your income.

It's great to live in a free country. If you don't like the weather where you live, you can take a vacation trip and dislike the weather there also.

A noted medical authority prescribes at least a week in the winter and a minimum of two weeks in the summer for his over-50 executive patients. Hard work alone probably never killed anyone, but failure to vary the routine can certainly make you stale and even undermine your health.

I once heard this statement about a man leaving for a vacation: "Vacation's a waste of time for him. I pity his poor wife and children if they think he's going to have fun with them. He's not a man; he's a civil war." There are a lot of people who carry their own private wars with them on vacation. For them recreation becomes wreck-reation.

A nice couple lying on the beach in Florida were discussing their children back home.

"D'you realize, Harvey," breathed the woman dreamily, "this is the first time we've been away without the kids?"

"Yeah," answered the husband. "I kinda miss them, Lucille--throw some sand in my face!"

## Watts New?

With the predominance of the home freezer, the home-from-work greeting has changed from "What's cooking?" to "What's thawing?" Technology leaves its trademark on every passing generation.

Isn't progress amazing? A grandmother was trying to teach some toddlers an old favorite song, "This is the way we wash our clothes," accompanied by washboard motions. It didn't go over! Not one of the modern small fry knew what a washboard was, though several could demonstrate tumble action in an automatic machine.

Mankind's constantly changing lifestyle even gives a lift to Mother Nature. Grocery stores, drug stores, and feed stores carry bags of ready-mixed bird seed. Now here is a sign of the times. A few years ago most folks were willing to crumble up stale bread and table scraps and put it out for the birds. Today we have fancy packaging and clever advertising for everything--some of it strictly for the birds!

The air waves constantly beam into our homes news of the newest. The main idea in television is to provide, as cheaply and easily as possible, something to fill the time between commercials. Do you know what happened to the children whose parents used to complain because they listened to the radio too much? They've grown up to be grandparents who complain that today's children watch too much television.

Maybe you can blame this on television: There was a guy who wanted to encourage some musical talent in his children, so he bought them a piano. When he got home they were contemplating the piano in puzzlement. "How," they asked, "do you plug it in?"

We live in a world of advertising. One restaurant is offering "New Improved Old-Fashioned Beef Stew," and a retail jeweler has a sign in his window, "Cuckoo Clocks Psychoanalyzed."

But all housemakers aren't gullible. A salesman was trying to sell an egg timer. "Your husband's eggs will be just right if you use this," he assured the woman. "But I don't need it," she answered brightly. "Jack likes his eggs the way I do them. I just look through the window at the traffic lights and give them three reds and two greens."

Someone gave me a Water Pic--that's an electric toothbrush that squirts. Unfortunately, I have wind-up teeth. Remember the good old days, when radios plugged in and toothbrushes didn't? I have one of those Early American toothbrushes. It comes with a key, a kite, and it only works during thunderstorms. When they made them with batteries, the major cause of halitosis became weak batteries.

Did you ever expect to see the day when you'd make a down payment on a toothbrush (that squirts)? But it is an ingenious device. Our five-year-old granddaughter was squirting the Water Pic in a glass. I said, "What's that?" She said, "A Pepsodent malted!"

But it's wonderful owning a Water Pic. A lot of people think cleaning your teeth with an electrically-powered stream of water is silly, but it isn't. Along with the electric dishwasher, the electric can opener, and the electric shoehorn, it's become a vital part of the American scene.

Right now in our bathroom, we have the new electric dental device (that squirts), an electric razor, an electric sun lamp, an electric hair dryer, an electric massager. We have more controls in the john than they used to get Frankenstein swinging. Never mind asking, can your wife cook? What does she know about fuses? A real catch as a spouse today isn't a homemaker. It's an electrical engineer!

You know how wars start? Take a wife with an electric coffeemaker, a husband with an electric razor, a son with an electric guitar, and a daughter with an electric hair dryer --and put 'em all together in a room with one outlet.

Pretty soon we're going to be a transistorized, battery-operated, muscleless society. We know a kid that was given a bat for his birthday and he wanted to know where it's batteries were.

I can see it now. Hundreds of years from now, archaeologists will poke around in the dust trying to determine what caused the decline and fall of the American civilization--and all they will find is a battery-operated pepper mill.

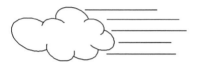

## *Weather Or Not*

In the southwestern sunshine you can't judge a woman by her clothes. Insufficient evidence.

Everybody talks about the weather. A native of Nevada went back East and was boasting at length of this state's fine climate and scenic beauties. "Why gentlemen," said he, "all Nevada needs is more water and a little better class of people."

Came the quick answer--"Man, that's all hell needs!"

In the country, as at sea, the great drama of life is supplied by the elements. The sky is man's protagonist. Wind, rain, drought, blizzards play across the farmland. People wax or wane in rhythm with the meteorologic visitations. No city person can feel the farmer's interest in the weather.

City folks get locked in on their thermostats. Temperature is always a problem at Senior Citizens Centers. You're never quite sure which is going to win out--the cool of the air conditioning or the heat from birthday cakes.

Tempers flare in those apartment houses where they can't agree on the thermostat. My uncle lives in a condominium where everything is done by committee. One time they had a fire and the vote was 32 to 7 to call the fire department--the seven that voted against were people who wanted more heat.

Professor Clarence S. Mills, University of Cincinnati, says there are a number of atmospheric conditions which, individually and collectively, affect human moods. Weather changes, barometric pressures, temperatures, electricity, and sunspots among them.

Human relationships everywhere would be more peaceful and unruffled if people would only realize the effect of weather on their dispositions and make proper allowances for little flareups, says Professor Mills.

Maybe he's right. The next time I feel like blowing my stack I'll first call my favorite TV weatherman!

## *Women*

According to a dress expert, the new fashions in clothes have caused women to reveal more femininity. It seems that bit by bit our women are losing their manhood. One reason why it is hard to understand a woman is because she never wants to make herself plain. Bless their hearts, they are ever in extremes; they are either better or worse than men. They were made before mirrors and have been before them ever since. Why is it we never hear of a self-made woman?

A woman is a person who can hurry through a drug-store aisle 18 inches wide without brushing against the piled-up tinware and then drive home and knock the doors off a 12-foot garage. The modern girl admires spinning wheels, but she wants four of them and a spare. Woman's complete emancipation will never come until some genius has perfected a home that can be run by a steering wheel, a clutch, and a brake.

In telling her age a woman is often shy in more ways than one. The best way to tell a woman's age is a mistake. The woman is young who does not look a day older than she says she is.

The census reports widows are twice as numerous as widowers. This seems to confirm the belief that women learn quicker than men.

Among the jurors summoned for a trial was a woman who wished to be excused. "Well, madam, why don't you want to serve on this jury?" asked the judge.

"I'm opposed to capital punishment."

"But this is merely a case in which a wife is suing her husband for an account. It seems she gave him a thousand dollars to pay down on a beautiful coat, and he is alleged to have lost the money at poker."

The woman juror spoke up promptly, "I'll serve. Maybe I'm wrong about capital punishment."

Some women feel they would just as well make a fool out of a man as to let some other woman do it, and when she says she can read you like a book, you can be sure she sees your finish. Some say, "Woman's place is in the home"--especially on the evenings when she brings home her paycheck!

# *Work*

This country will always have several million unemployed looking for work wherever they know they can't find it. So many people are busy being unemployed that it's getting hard to get any work done. Many people want jobs, but not as many want work.

Personally we don't know the secret of success, but we are afraid it's work. Despite the efforts to find a substitute, elbow grease is still the essential oil of industry. The spirit of unrest that makes the world go 'round is the spirit of work. Work, of course, is the cure for unrest, but there are lots of people who think the remedy is worse than the disease.

America has always been a land of opportunity where a family can progress in one generation from a plain cabin to a cabin plane, but today too many people think opportunity means a chance to get money without earning it. More people get crooked from trying to avoid hard work than become bent from too much of it.

Whatever happened to the guy who met the wolf at the door and appeared the next day with a fur coat? Or the river valley farmer who turned cheerfully from corn to frogs? A good deal of our laziness of mind today is called "liberty of opinion"--it's the opinion that it is the government's responsibility to take care of everybody. Now we are raising a generation whose parents have always been on the dole and they certainly have concrete opinions--thoroughly mixed and permanently set. The reason they can't hear opportunity knocking is because they are busy knocking the opportunities.

- 152 -

I like to recall the story about a visitor to a part of Maryland not noted for its fertile soil. The visitor watched an old patriarch laboring with his son and two grandsons in a cabbage patch. It was hard to find the young plants among the rocks. The visitor spoke to the old man and inquired, "Tell me, what can you raise in these rocky hills?"

The old man gave the visitor a withering look. Then he straightened up. Slowly he wiped the back of one gnarled, sweated fist across his firm lips, and he fairly spat out his answer, "Men!"

## *World Peace*

Hostile feelings now flaring within nations are enough to make the dove of peace a little cuckoo.

The big nations around the world are insisting so fiercely that they want peace that there may be a war over who wants it most. Leaders of the big nations are determined not to let the little ones fight; perhaps they should settle their own problems.

It took a wise old Indian to discover why the leaders of the most important nations of the world cannot get together on any settlement when they gather for their conferences. "The trouble is," observed the Indian, "everybody smokes the peace pipe, but nobody inhales."

It would be nice to be able to say that the whole world longs and yearns for peace. We need to understand that this is just not so. There are people in the world who are still delighted with the business of war. Rising nationalism and noisy voices overwhelm the cries for peace.

The only real obstacle to everlasting peace is the fact that there are more dogs than bones, and if universal peace is ever established, two-thirds of the world is going to get caught entirely unprepared for it.

The two fearful possibilities threatening world peace are (1) a big war, and (2) a big peace conference. The big idea of a peace conference is to find out who won't win the next war. A common interest would keep the nations at peace, and even common honesty would help. Peace is a state of mind--of mind your own business. Too many men strive for peace with their fists clenched.

Depending on diplomacy for peace reminds us of the man who wears a hat until he becomes bald and then he wears a hat to hide his baldness.

Every once in a while we hear of an organization launched to work for international peace. There are some people who think that all nations should get along like one big family. The trouble is that they do!

We are a peace-loving people, seldom paying pensions for more than three wars at a time, and in spite of all the propaganda for world peace, there probably will be the usual number of weddings in June.

There's just one sure way to find peace--hunt it up in your Funk & Wagnall's.

It would be great if wars could be solved at the conference table, but I've never heard of a monument to the Unknown Diplomat.

You can depend on the fact that the great oil reserves will be subject to militancy for years to come. I have this recurring nightmare: American scientists perfect solar power. Then the Arabs buy the sun. You know what would add another interesting dimension to the Mideast problem? If someone invented a car that ran on chicken soup.

It's hard to say where world events are leading, but the latest history books list World War I, World War II, and Watch This Space! I'll tell you how bad things are. You know those fellas who march with signs saying THE END IS NEAR? I saw two of them synchronizing their watches. I know a guy who's building an ark--and no one's laughing.

Nuclear radiation has everyone shook up. Nobody can be sure what long-term effect nuclear radiation has on people. My Uncle Willie worked in a nuclear power plant for 15 years, put in for early retirement and just last week started a second career in Portland, Maine--as a lighthouse. Fortunately, there are always little tell-tale signs when you are exposed to radiation. For instance, your pocket calculator no longer run on batteries--it runs on you!

# Worry

It doesn't pay to worry. If you went through last year's file marked "Important"--chances are the only things you'd keep are the paper clips. Worry, tension, and depression are becoming modern killers. Everybody's up tight. My neighbor is depressed about the human race. He wants to sue God for malpractice. There's even a new tranquilizer--it doesn't relax you, but it makes you feel good about being up tight.

The roamers of yesterday's frontier world would be the misfits of today. What saved them was plenty of room to do their shooting in. You could kill a buffalo and be a hero. Man has a harder time adjusting now because there are more people, closer together. You can stand anyone if you're not with him too much. And that's what mental health is all about; man adjusting to man.

Too many people don't face difficulties as they come along. They let them accumulate until they blow up.

Life is a lot like wearing bifocals. There are two ways to look at almost anything. For instance, when it comes to our checking account I say my wife is overdrawn. She says I'm underdeposited.

Handling difficulty, making the best of bad messes, is one of life's major jobs. Often the reason success is not achieved in solving a problem lies inside the individual; we just don't dissect the problem and look at it one piece at a time. At times we all resemble the farmer laboriously driving his horses on a dusty road. "How much longer does this hill last?" he asked a man by the side of the road. "Hill!" was the answer. "Hill nothing! Your hind wheels are off!"

Norman Vincent Peale, minister, author, and columnist, looks at it this way, "A person with a hundred interests is twice as alive as one with only 50 and four times as alive as the man who has only 25. What are you interested in--food, home, business, clothes, family? If you want to be free from nervous tension and live a healthier life, you should widen your interests, broaden yourself."

If you feel like a tap dancer in the canoe of life, maybe it's your own fault!

## *Wrong Number*

Ten years ago, did you ever think you'd be reading in bed by the light of the telephone?--It's little! It's lovely! It lights! It's polite--it only speaks when spoken to.

There's a telephone operator in Chinatown who's all shook up. Keeps getting Wong numbers.

Do you realize if Alexander Graham Bell hadn't invented the telephone, we'd all be sitting around waiting for the bridge lamp to ring?

I can't understand the telephone company. I came up with a great idea to make life simpler for customers, and the company's just ignoring it--a directory for unlisted numbers.

Did you know the telephone company is now using men as operators? Neither did I until I got one on the phone. I said, "I'd like to talk to an operator." He said, "I am an operator." I said, "How do I know you're an operator?" He said, "I'm alone with 85 women, aren't I?"

Personally, I think the phone company should add a little sex appeal to its operation. Like calling the people in Directory Assistance informaniacs.

A loser is someone who phones a number on a washroom wall--and it's Dial-A-Prayer.

I like to think deep philosophical thoughts--like, how does an obscene caller know when he gets a wrong number?

I won't say my wife gossips, but at our house opportunity has to knock. If it phoned, it'd get a busy signal.

You know what's nice about all those recorded phone messages? You can finally tell the operator what she can do with her advice.

Last month I got a bill for $83. Who could talk that much? Either the bill is wrong or the parakeet's learned how to dial.

If you've had any experiences with the employees at answering services, you know anything after "hello" comes hard for them. They're not the brightest bulbs in the circuit.

# Jack Lacy Always "Left 'Em Laughing"

Author, nationally-known public speaker and newspaper columnist Jack Lacy appeared on hundreds of speaker platforms. His rapid-fire wit kept audiences "gasping for breath," one reviewer said.

Before his death from cancer in late 1994, Lacy compiled his collection of one-liners, stories and wisecracks into a book called S.H.O.R.T.S. Lacy's friend, Senate Majority Leader Bob Dole says it combines "savvy and common sense."

"I never refused an invitation to speak," Lacy said. His audiences ranged from 20 to 2,000, but he always declined a fee.

Lacy came from a career as a Colorado newspaper man before entering organization management in La Junta, Colorado. He went on to manage Chambers of Commerce in St. Joseph, Pueblo and Amarillo before entering professional economic development work for the states of New Mexico and Kansas. He directed the Kansas Association of Commerce and Industry and served as president of the Junction City Chamber of Commerce. Lacy is listed in Who's Who in America, Who's Who in World Commerce and Industry.

He honed his humor writing a column, "Viva Trivia," for the Rio Rancho, New Mexico *Observer.*

Laughing can be good for your liver, doctors tell us. If they're right, Jack Lacy has left a healing trail through New Mexico, Texas and Kansas. His book, S.H.O.R.T.S., now extends that tonic guffaw to readers everywhere.

*For each man with a spark of genius there are 10 with ignition trouble...*Humorist and speaker Jack Lacy.

Order Gift Copies of S.H.O.R.T.S. By Mail!

___      copies of S.H.O.R.T.S. @ $9.95 ea.   _____

Colorado tax @ .03   (.30 ea.)       _____
Denver Metro tax @.038   (.38 ea.)   _____
Postage & Handling @ $2.00 ea.    _____

Send to:    Triple J Press
               3154 E. Longs Circle S.
               Littleton, CO  80122
               (303) 779-0033

Name _____
Address_____
City _____ State ____ ZIP _____